The Price of Profit

Printed by: Amazon Kindle Direct Publishing

ISBN-13: 978-1980349051

First Print: February 2018

THE PRICE OF PROFIT

Jason Wicks

For Charlotte,

"When the winds of change blow, some people build walls, others build windmills"

- *Chinese Proverb*

Contents

Introduction

Ever since our ancestors wandered around the planet thousands of years ago, competition has played a sizable part in the evolutionary process that followed. Natural selection's sole 'job', if we anthropomorphise it, was simply to ensure that our genes were passed down to the next generation. In the times of our ancestors, physical superiority may have increased a man's chances of reproduction, as would greater access to natural resources. Competition, whether we like it or not, had its purpose throughout our evolution, and it's undoubtedly a contributing factor to the quality of life we can enjoy today.

However, thousands and thousands of years ago, reproduction was not necessarily a given. Not every single person was successful in passing on their genes, hence why overcoming competition was necessary for our ancestors to manage it. This scenario was particularly the case for males, following our 'invention' of an agricultural system. A study of reproduction in humans 8000 years ago found that for every one man that successfully managed to pass on their genes, 17 women were able to do the same. What this suggests is that a select few men would reproduce with multiple women, while the rest may never reproduce at all. The study speculated that this startling statistic was potentially the result of some men gaining an abundance of wealth and power, leaving other men with very little. The ones that had it had women queuing up to sleep with them, while those that didn't would be stuck on an ancestral merry-go-round of fruitless first dates.

Fast forward to the 21st century, and you'll notice similar behaviour, but without the underlying purpose that drove our ancestors to compete. When we think about it, virtually everybody's genes are successfully making it to the next generation, irrespective of a multitude of factors, including wealth. However, our brains don't seem to have yet caught up with this realisation, and our constant drive to accumulate power and money seems as tribal as ever. Having never studied psychology, let alone evolutionary psychology, this is where the science stops and the rest of the book begins. When applying these concepts to business and consumerism, you don't need a degree to look around and directly observe how people are behaving.

I remember being a young child at the point in my life where I was just about old enough to understand that being a superhero or spy wasn't a realistic career plan. As I sought after more viable alternatives, my natural instinct was to try and find something that would provide me with the most money, for the least effort, which tells you all you need to know about my work ethic. In all seriousness, I refuse to believe that this ambition was in anyway uncommon. We have been so conditioned to value financial reward, that it has become one of the most significant factors in our decision making. How many people, for example, would actively choose to continue working in their current job if they won the lottery? How many people genuinely enjoy what they do to the point where their intrinsic motivation dwarfs the extrinsic incentive that a salary provides?

There are endless theories that try explain this innate desire, but I think it predominantly comes down to how we view and value success. Whether we like to think about it or not, we all know deep down that we won't be around forever. We know that our time on this planet is little more than an infinitely small dot on the timeline of the Earth. In fact, if I drew the said timeline, and the average person's life was the final centimetre of it, then the start would have to be nearly 600km away. Like it or not, in the grand scheme of things, we are all completely insignificant. It is this knowledge that has created the notion that we have to make the best of our brief time here. Don't get me wrong, I'm not suggesting that the thought of our mortality is so present in our minds that every action is in some way a result of trying to make the most of life, but it has no doubt influenced modern society as we know it. Generally speaking, we are attached to the idea that we need to prove that our life hasn't been a waste of time. Most of us if asked, will also admit to liking the idea of leaving a 'legacy', something that will live on after we cease to be.

The problem with success is that it's extremely tough for us to measure and be sure of. If I'm going to dedicate my entire existence to living fully and then leaving this profound and enduring legacy, I'm going to need a measuring system to know when I'm on the right track, right? Similarly, I'm also going to need to compare my success with that of my peers, again to justify whether it's all been worthwhile. The last thing I would want is to spend 50 years trying to make the most of my stint on Earth, only to find out that Dave down the road has achieved more than I have in a fraction of the time. Comparison, and therefore competition (remember that?), is essential.

This underlying challenge is where the idea of money comes in. Money, by definition, allows us to quantify our achievements and compare them to those of others, and I firmly believe that it is this function that makes it so desirable. Of course, the irony of this desire is that in our quest for external and superficial gratification we fail to reach the heights that internal satisfaction can elevate us to. However, like all forms of material gratification, money merely serves as a makeshift catapult to contentment, a sudden rush of pleasure which vanishes as quickly as it arises. From that point on our 'addiction' takes hold, and our desire for wealth gets stronger and stronger while the rush of satisfaction gets weaker every time.

If these ideas interest you, then I have some bad news, as they are not what this book is about. This book isn't a self-help guide or a handbook for a more peaceful living. What I'm interested in primarily, is the consequences of this desire. With wealth so highly regarded and sought after, we very rarely stop and realise that for us to accumulate it, somebody else has to lose it. Now there is nothing inherently wrong with that, as everybody gains and loses money and some people get more than others if they work harder or take higher risks that pay off. That's essentially how our system operates, and while we could no doubt refine it significantly, I don't think we should abandon it altogether. After all, if I go to work, I deserve to be paid for the effort I put in, and the fact that the company employing me technically 'loses' the money they give me is not exactly a negative consequence because they gain my productivity.

When looking at things on an individual level in this manner, the consequences of wealth accumulation, while still existent, are pretty meaningless and mundane. However, when we start to turn our attention to broader levels of activity, that conclusion no longer holds. An example of this is when we begin to observe what goes on in organisations. After all, businesses are merely groups of people coming together to achieve a common goal, and if people value wealth and power so highly, then it stands to reason that for the most part, organisations won't behave any differently. The only change this time around is that with more resources and a broader scope of impact, the potential consequences of their actions range from significant to catastrophic. That is what this book is about.

Let's take the global organisation, Apple, as an example. As of 2017, Apple employs over 120,000 people worldwide. They operate in as many countries as you can name and have sold millions and millions of products. The scope of their activity is unquestionably extreme. As a result, the consequences of their profit maximisation take some truly dark and disturbing turns. For starters, most of the metals contained within your everyday smartphone are extracted in countries with traditionally high levels of poverty, in conditions where worker's lives are almost invariably at risk. Then comes product assembly. In the Foxconn factory in Longhua, China, electronic items are manufactured and assembled for a variety of companies, including Apple. Working conditions were so poor, and pay was so low that, in 2010, workers started killing themselves by jumping from windows and stairwells. The harrowing response to such a situation, was the installation of nets that were hung on the outer walls of the building, to catch any workers trying to take their own life.

This apparent systemic failure leaves us with multiple questions and problems that we must attempt to navigate. Firstly, how do we quantify these consequences? How can we start to understand where the acceptable limit of profit maximisation lies? Finally, and perhaps most challengingly, how can we ensure that the economic system we adopt incentivises behaviour that benefits society and discourages immorality? The remainder of this book will attempt to answer some of these questions, as well as highlight the difficulties associated with implementing any of the solutions. After all, let's not forget that the example of Apple is merely one of many companies and the treatment of workers is one of many negative consequences. In truth, organisations all around the world are directly contributing to social issues such as inequality and low quality of life, as well as environmental issues such as resource scarcity and global warming. The cause and effect relationship is there for us all to see; we just need to look in the right places. While the current situation may seem somewhat murky by nature, the one thing that seems abundantly clear, and will be talked about in more depth in later chapters, is that something needs to change.

Perhaps the crux of this problem is that despite our somewhat miraculous evolutionary journey to the present day, we aren't particularly receptive to change. For whatever reason, our natural instinct seems to be to maintain the status quo. Even significant events that appear to offer change, such as elections and referendums, are in some way illusory. Both possible outcomes of the Brexit vote, for example, would still exist within the same systemic economic parameters that have governed us in recent memory. It's this mindset that distances us from what is possible, resigning ourselves to the role of a passive observer within society. Inherently, this is quite ironic. With the world constantly changing at a pretty rapid rate, it seems entirely counterproductive to try and continually resist it. As the Greek philosopher, Heraclitus once said, "Life is flux", a quote that has since been understood to suggest that 'the only constant is change itself'. When we think about it, everything is constantly changing to such an extent that change itself is the only thing we can rely on. Perhaps by acknowledging, accepting and embracing this, we can seek new ways of doing things, ways which could positively influence the society we belong to.

I think it's important at this point to address a critical misconception when it comes to understanding (and potentially changing) the way organisations operate. There is a temptation to misconstrue these ideas as attacks on businesses or business owners. In reality, this is far from the case. The way I prefer to look at it, and the way I feel more accurately depicts the situation is by thinking of these issues as systemic problems. The way our society is set up has thrust businesses into the role of the pantomime villain, while consumers make up the paying audience, continually indulging in the entire facade. When we look at companies such as Apple, we must appreciate that their products aren't necessarily the problem because Apple themselves are a product of a broader issue.

This metaphor doesn't mean that organisations are always irresponsible in some way or another. On the contrary, I genuinely believe that they hold all the cards that contain the necessary solutions. All that we need to do is tell them how they should be played. The thing is, in the time it has taken you to read this short introduction, approximately ten new start-ups will have been registered in the UK alone. Over the next five years, only four or five of those original ten will still be operating, but by that time another three million will have been created. These 'birth' rates are growing too, so the slightly depressing survival prospects don't put many budding entrepreneurs off pursuing their dream to become the next Bill Gates.

With these stats in mind, we face a rather simple choice. On the one hand, we do nothing, let nature take its course and try and sort out any negative consequences of profit maximisation as and when they arise. On the other hand, we see these facts as a cause for excitement, as an untapped power source for societal change that all we need to do is harness. That's not to suggest that doing so is easy, but I certainly think it's worth trying.

1

Cash Mountain

Why do some people decide to start a business? This is a question that seems relatively straightforward, and in many ways it is, but it's one that we need to be prepared to explore if we want to make some headway with this idea of using corporate power as a genuine driver of social good. In the introduction, I spoke about the role of money in our society and our continued desire for it. Maybe this is the simple answer to the above question? It makes sense that, if we want to be rich and powerful, owning a thriving business is a pretty good first step towards leaving a genuine mark on the world. This answer is in no means illogical, and there is almost certainly a financial component behind anyone's decision to start a business, but is there a chance that maybe, just maybe, there's a little bit more to it?

I like to think that this is something most people would agree on. Sure, owning a business can reward you financially in ways that working for somebody else never will, but if all you're looking to do is make money, then a business is probably not your best option. For starters, it takes an extraordinary amount of work, a generous helping of luck, and even then there is no guarantee that you'll still be operating in five years. If you're after a get rich quick scheme, it's almost certain that starting your own business isn't it. You don't have to look too far for proof of just how difficult it is either. If I asked you what you think Amazon, ESPN and Tesla all have in common; you might not realise that they are all companies that didn't make a single pound of profit for the first five years of their existence.

So outside of financial incentives, what are some other reasons to start a business? Well, I recently stumbled across a blog article that asked this exact question to multiple entrepreneurs, and the responses were the kind of heart-warming insights into people's motivations that you would like to expect. While several individuals acted because they weren't very good at taking orders from somebody else, there were also cases of people looking to 'turn their hobby into a profession'. However, the answers that particularly grabbed my attention all shared a specific and common theme; they wanted to use their expertise and enthusiasm to help provide something to other people who needed it.

This answer to me is the essence of what business is about, and it's no doubt responsible, at least in part, for so much of the progress we have enjoyed as a society over the past decades. I'm sure when tech companies like Microsoft started out, there was an element of wanting to see what was possible and see how their expertise could help people. I doubt Bill Gates set out to become the wealthiest man in the world, with Microsoft just being his chosen strategy for doing so. If these more abstract motivations for business owners are so common and socially beneficial, why then, are we in a situation were profit maximisation is destroying the planet and ruining the lives for so many people that live on it? This issue is why I felt the need to ask the question in the first place.

The way I see it, regardless of why a business came into being, as it grows in size and becomes more and more complex, the primary objective soon becomes maximising profits. Don't get me wrong, businesses need to make profits to survive, and if they are providing consumers with a product or service that improves their quality of life, then it's in our best interest to keep them going. However, why is it that so often, the pursuit of profit results in a disregard for the underlying relationship between the business and its customers? As the quest profit maximisation intensifies, customers become little more than statistics and data, things that companies can easily manipulate into parting with as much of their money as possible. Take a moment to think about some of the companies you buy from on a daily basis. How many of those companies would you say value and understand you as a consumer, and how many would you admit are just after your money? Of course, all businesses are after your money some way or another, but there are definitely times where we can feel the relationship goes beyond that. On that point, do you notice that the ones that genuinely care are usually smaller than the ones that don't?

Now, we can't merely say that small companies are great and big companies are evil, as that wouldn't get us anywhere. What we can do, however, is understand the role that profit plays as a company grows, as it may help us realise what goes on behind the scenes. In reality, it doesn't take a genius to figure it out.

With smaller companies, survival is less of a guarantee. They don't have the resources to survive any fluctuations in demand that could be caused by releasing a product that doesn't sell for example, or even external factors such as recessions. When survival is the primary objective, every customer and contract matters, and every piece of feedback is invaluable. Yes, they want your money, but they're willing to build a genuine relationship with you in order to get it. With larger companies however, the threat of survival is far less of a concern. Occasionally a big company will suffer a dramatic set back that forces them into liquidation, such as Monarch Airlines in the UK, but for the most part, survival is pretty much assumed. The second that companies take survival for granted, their objectives shift towards things such as growth, market share, and ultimately profit.

In essence, there is nothing wrong with companies making decent profits. If I feel that a company is making a product that makes my life better, then there's no reason for me to begrudge them a financial reward for doing so. What's more, the money I give them can then be used to make more things that will make both my life and the lives of others even better in the future. I think this is a part of the customer-business exchange that is often overlooked. Consider the act of buying a new phone for £300. While on the face of it you are saying that the phone is worth £300, you're also implying that the phone company deserves the profit for providing you with it. Even more subconsciously, however, you are also saying that you approve of how they are operating and essentially want them to be able to continue doing so. It can be quite easy as consumers not to realise or appreciate that this is effectively what we are doing every time we make a purchase.

Again, it is important to stress that so far, there is nothing intrinsically undesirable about this. One of the main arguments in favour of profit maximisation is simply that, by striving for it, companies are contributing to our economy (through jobs and taxes etc.) and making all of our lives better. The question is, what happens if the necessary level of tax isn't paid? What happens if the jobs created are exploitative? We must be prepared to admit that, sometimes, profit can cause a lot of societal damage. However, if this is the case, why is it that we let these negative things happen? Going back to the original purchasing transaction, I think this is a result of one (or sometimes both) of the following scenarios:

a) Companies maximise profit by doing things that we don't approve of but without us knowing, meaning we still buy from them.

b) Companies fail to use the profit we have 'given' them in a way that we would've hoped/expected. Again, without us knowing that that's what they were planning to do.

Examples of a) are, unfortunately, plentiful. One of the biggest issues surrounding larger organisations is that there are so many layers and stages that go into the product we decide to buy. As the size of the company increases, it becomes almost impossible to truly acknowledge and understand what our purchasing decision is ultimately 'approving' of. If every consumer knew every detail behind the production of every product, I'm sure we would behave rather differently. Sadly, examples of b) are plentiful too, and as I've just mentioned, tax evasion is a particularly relevant one. When we spend money on a product, we, albeit subconsciously, hope that said money is being fairly used and distributed. Part of that distribution should be paying the correct amount of corporation tax. I'm not an iPhone user myself, but I'd resent having paid £1000 for the new iPhone X, only to find out that the company has $250bn stashed away in offshore accounts so that they don't have to pay any tax on it. All while the people who assemble them try and take their own lives.

In all fairness to Apple, and I have mentioned them a few times already, in January 2018 they announced that they planned to move their offshore 'cash mountain' back to the U.S., resulting in a tax bill of $38bn. Unfortunately, the inconvenient truth is that Apple, in this instance at least, are more of an exception than the rule itself, and numerous multinational organisations are involved in similar strategies to reduce their tax bill.

While a) and b) are both very much the start of a socially detrimental pursuit of profit, we must acknowledge why such a situation has been able to go on for so long. As you will no doubt have noticed, the one thing that both a) and b) have in common is the idea of asymmetric information. All this really means is that one side of the transaction (in this case the company) has far more information than the other party (the consumer). As a singular entity, 'the company' knows the harm they may be causing, while the customer is largely none the wiser. This difference in knowledge gives corporations a vast amount of power. In essence, it means that many companies will, for the most part, do what they can get away with, as long as consumers don't find out about it.

I think this is a good time to reiterate the pantomime villain analogy I offered up in the introduction. When I suggest that companies do whatever they can get away with, I'm not trying to insinuate that somewhere in an Apple Board meeting Tim Cook turns round on his throne-like swivel chair stroking a fluffy white cat before suggesting that they stop paying tax. Instead, I'm highlighting my earlier point that the current system makes such a strategy a viable, and often necessary, option.

Realistically, it probably worked as follows: Apple tried to save some money on their tax bill, nobody kicked up much of a fuss, so they kept doing it. Even now when people have started questioning the morality of their actions, they casually move the money back to the U.S., pay the tax bill and put it down as a lesson learnt. For whatever reason, I don't think I would be allowed to adopt the same trial and error philosophy for my tax return.

This concept then leads to a somewhat daunting realisation. If companies are too powerful for governments to regulate and monitor efficiently, and if they are free to adopt their own set of rules that individuals can't follow, where does this leave ordinary consumers? It's at this point where any notion of 'people power' appears unattainable. If organisations are effectively above the law because any fine they may be given is so negligible in the grand scheme of things, it's too easy for us to hand over a blank cheque to these companies, letting them behave however they like. This problem is precisely what I think has taken place throughout the past decade, and as I have already touched upon and will explore in more detail later, the consequences are severe.

Taking a few steps back from the tangent of taxation, I'd like to pick up on the idea of profit maximising and the mechanics of why it's something that at some point or another starts to dominate corporate ambition. It all links back to this evolutionary desire for being successful and outcompeting those around us. As we have established, money is a primary way in which we can do that, and I can't help but think it behaves quite like a drug in many ways, particularly when you look at our addiction to it. As a company becomes profitable, there is an innate desire to always better their previous level of success. You will very rarely see companies, particularly on a global scale, that are happy plodding along at a certain level. This is obviously because unless every rival company simultaneously decided to cap their growth, they'd soon find themselves in a fair bit of financial trouble. However, such a situation wouldn't be desirable to society anyway when you consider that competition promotes innovation that makes our lives better as a result. No consumers would want any company to be standing still for too long. But, as companies continuously try to improve performance, it becomes harder and harder for them to manage it. There's only so cheaply you can manufacture something, and there's only so much you can sell it for. This is the issue.

The thing is, as profits increase, so too do the shareholder's expectations, which put more pressure on increasing profit, which raises expectations even further. Quite a sizable problem in a capitalist system is the reliance on, and the hope of, unlimited growth from limited resources. The negative consequences that we are currently able to observe are little more than a signal of the strain that organisations are presently experiencing when trying to generate their next 'fix' of profit. It works in a very similar way to emerging/developing economies. There are countries on the planet that are experiencing rapid annual growth of around 10% a year. As a result, citizens, investors and the global community start to expect and even count on that level of growth to be sustained. The effect of this is that when the economy inevitably struggles to maintain their previous growth level, the consequences can be severe. A country that goes from 10% growth in one year to 2% growth in the next could experience economic downturns similar to that of a recession, even though the economy is still technically growing. Profit works in a similar way, and firms whose profits are down on the year before are seen as monumental failures, even if they're still making millions of pounds.

I don't want you to think that I'm massively overdramatising the role of profit to fit a specific narrative, so I'll introduce the work of a famous economist Milton Friedman. Friedman is known, perhaps controversially so, for his view that the only responsibility an organisation has is to maximise profit, in whichever way they deem necessary. Friedman is one of the most well-known economists in modern times, and in saying the above statement, he effectively ruled out the idea that organisations have any altruistic obligations to society. Going back a few pages when I asked the question of why people start businesses, I imagine Friedman's view would be considered the logical extension of the idea that the sole purpose of starting a business is the potential for financial and economic gain. Even if the original reasons to start up were something more intrinsic such as helping people, Friedman would suggest that from that point on, you should only help people if it maximises profits, as opposed to profit being a mere by-product of helping people.

Friedman's approach is, however, just one of many when it comes to the responsibilities and obligations of businesses. A particularly popular converse opinion, and the one that underpins this entire book is referred to as the stakeholder approach. While Friedman focusses exclusively on returns for shareholders, academics such as Ian Mitroff and R. Edward Freeman (which is admittedly confusing with his name being very similar to Friedman) argue that businesses should consider a broader range of 'stakeholders'. These academics weren't necessarily the first to pose such arguments, but they did so at a time when corporate social responsibility was slowly starting to become a recognised practice. In short, they argued that stakeholders are anybody who is affected in any way by the operational activity of an organisation. For example, suppliers, local community residents, employees, governments and customers are all types of different stakeholders. When a business chooses to adopt this approach, they may find they suddenly have more responsibilities and obligations than they first anticipated, but it certainly maximises their ability to influence society more positively.

The distinction between the two views can be demonstrated with a simple example. Imagine you own a small bakery in the middle of a busy town. If your only concerns were shareholders and profit, you'd buy the cheapest ingredients you could get away with, pay staff as little as you could get away with and sell everything at the highest price you can get away with, not spending too much time worrying about the morality of doing so. On the flipside, a bakery adopting a stakeholder approach might wish to make sure that their suppliers are suitably paid. They may want to source ingredients locally to help sustain businesses in their local area, and they may choose to offer a small discount to any residents that live close enough to be disrupted by the production noises in the early hours of the morning.

Now, of these two approaches, which one will probably enable the owner to make the most profit? Given our current system and the idea of asymmetric information, it would probably be the first one. However, what if the owner of the bakery only wants to earn a modest living from doing what he/she loves? What if, to them, profit is only important up to a certain point, beyond which it's not particularly necessary? If that's the case, as long as the bakery survives and provides the owner with the modest income that they're after, the business is undeniably successful. Of course, this is a very particular, and hypothetical, example, and it would be quite naïve to suggest that the best solution to the problem of profit maximisation is to make sure that business owners measure success in other ways. Not only would such a suggestion never actually work, but it wouldn't be able to scale up when we look at companies that are larger than a local bakery. What I would encourage you to do however, is remember this hypothetical example, as it may come in handy when proposing what is unarguably the more viable solution.

Regardless of your personal opinion at this given moment, and the pros and cons associated with each approach, the stakeholder idea has stuck around ever since its introduction. Such is its success that it's pretty much viewed as the clear alternative to Friedman's original school of thought. Unfortunately, this is where it's started to become a bit of a corporate buzzword. In recent years, numerous different terms have been used to try and describe what is now a very credible business practice. Some say ethics; some say sustainability, and some use corporate social responsibility. To some extent, the exact words are secondary to the intent and meaning behind them.

In short, the very notion that organisations should care, at least partly, about something other than profits and that their obligations extend past financial prosperity is slowly entering into the mainstream view of business management. As the primary 'breakthrough' surrounds the responsibilities of organisations, I'll try and stick to the term 'Corporate Social Responsibility' throughout this book. There are additional reasons for doing so, such as the fact that most companies engaging in these activities have 'Corporate Social Responsibility' departments and perhaps most importantly, it's super easy to abbreviate (to CSR) which makes my life a bit easier.

As you might have already deduced from the endless different theories and terms, CSR has slowly developed a rather bizarre reputation. For many, it's seen as something extra that businesses have to start doing, as though the people that came up with it didn't realise that companies have more than enough to worry about without having to care for society at the same time. As a result, the very concept has been met with some degree of scepticism. Even in large companies with CSR departments, it can be quite a task convincing other business functions that the work you're doing is worthwhile. On top of that, there is a general consensus that for now at least, any CSR activities you engage in are in some way harmful to the firm's profitability. Again, even people who work for companies with CSR departments sometimes share this view, so it's not a question of lack of exposure. What I would say is that despite my unsurprising disagreement with these two viewpoints, I can completely understand how these opinions have come about, and I think that CSR academics and practitioners are far from immune to taking some of the blame. What I'm therefore going to attempt to do is address these two criticisms in a way that hopefully makes you realise (if you currently agree with them) that CSR isn't all that bad, and isn't as complicated as some people make it out to be.

"CSR is just more things for a business to worry about"

The first way to address this misconception is to identify that CSR isn't a to-do list of good deeds that busy business owners have to find the time to tick off. You can't suddenly 'complete' CSR; it goes a bit deeper than that. To put it simply, CSR can (and should) be to business what nonconformity is to hippies; "it's a lifestyle".

Secondly, and perhaps the more significant point to make, is that CSR doesn't need to be seen as an extension of our traditional view of how and why businesses operate. As I've gradually hinted at and introduced throughout this chapter, I think a more valuable way of looking at it is thinking of CSR as stripping back our current understanding to return to the root of the relationship between business and society. As I discussed right at the start of the chapter, companies don't merely exist to make money; they exist to help people in the world, push the boundaries of what is possible and change people's lives for the better. I can't help but think, perhaps naïvely, that even if money didn't exist, people would still want to use their experience and enthusiasm to help others. People would still want to get together and try and create new ways of doing things. I mentioned in the introduction the role that competition played during our evolution, but it's also important to reflect on something I deliberately omitted until now: collaboration. Of course, individual competition played a sizable role in natural selection, but numerous studies point to collaboration and co-operation as the key reasons why we have survived and thrived for as long as we have. Organisations at their very core are simply highly concentrated examples of collaboration, and CSR should be viewed as little more than the practice of extending this togetherness to involve society as a whole.

"CSR just takes away from a firm's profitability."

This statement is probably the more common of the two critiques, and that's potentially because it's more justifiable. In an environment where competitors might be cutting costs left right and centre, you might be in trouble if you start trying to please every stakeholder you can name. In all honesty, the notion that CSR can harm profitability carries a fair amount of truth, especially if you look at organisational behaviour over the last few decades. Take the clothing market as a prime example. The reason why Primark were able to steal so many customers away from competitors was that they were able to capitalise on the cheap labour in developing countries where working conditions were less of an issue. It is also highly likely that child labour played a part in manufacturing, due to the power that Primark had over suppliers to push down costs. At the time, firms that opted for more ethically sourced products were losing out, even though they were doing the 'right' thing.

However, there may be a light at the end of the tunnel. As CSR is growing in importance and companies are taking it more seriously, an exciting transition is occurring that might just change its very nature and ultimately eradicate the credibility of this criticism. To explain this, it's helpful to think of a timeline or a life cycle of CSR as a concept.

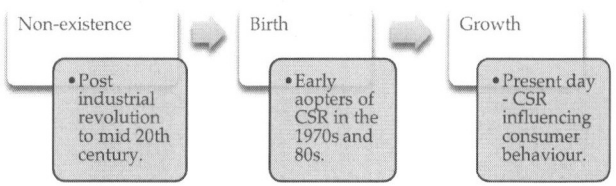

Following the industrial revolution, companies were able to take advantage of what seemed like a wealth of new resources, without the same awareness of their scarcity which exists today. At the same time, the world was less connected due to limited communication technology, so it was far harder to know how firms were behaving. Finally, due to the lack of the necessary information, the whole culture failed to place any real value on social and environmental responsibility. At this point, CSR was non-existent.

The second stage was the birth of CSR. What began as almost blue sky thinking in the 1930s gradually rose in popularity. However, even as landmark books were published in the 1950s, it wasn't until a bit later when CSR was taken seriously by some organisations. Realistically, it wasn't until the 1970s/80s that things started to change. People became more aware of social and environmental issues and valued them accordingly. The operational activity of businesses was more accessible to the public

than ever before, and transparency was becoming crucial. Some companies, perhaps unknowingly at the time, became 'Early Adopters' of CSR, using a particular social or environmental issue as a method of gaining a competitive advantage in the marketplace. The Body Shop is perhaps the best example of this. Founded in 1976, The Body Shop took the cosmetics industry by storm as a result of differentiating itself through its refusal to use animal testing. Another example was Ben & Jerry's, who became the first company to publish a social impact report in 1989. In general, consumers responded well to these types of businesses, and enough Early Adopters were successful to elevate CSR into a mainstream business practice.

Currently, we are in the third stage of the CSR life cycle, the 'teenage years' or 'growth' that arguably began around the turn of the millennium. Technological advances made acquiring information easier than ever, and the extent of any asymmetric information was reduced significantly. As a result, companies have quickly started to realise that CSR, in some form or another, is important to consumers. I'll drill down into some data later on, but numerous studies have pointed to the idea that the general public, especially the younger generations, will actively consider a company's CSR before making a purchase. What I think this does is hand power back to consumers, and position them somewhat at a moral crossroads of consumption. On the one hand, they can continue with their impulse spending, buying whatever they want as cheaply as they can get it, while putting any negative consequences out of mind. Alternatively, they can start to actively alter their spending patterns to reward business activities that they approve of. Doing this goes far beyond traditional boycotts, and instead focusses on ensuring that money only goes to the companies that most deserve it.

If enough people do this, and it certainly seems to be a growing trend, then the firms that are the most responsible will be the ones that make the most profit. This is the more viable solution that the one I alluded to earlier. Consumers don't necessarily have the power to make firms stop desiring profit, but they can set new benchmarks for what firms must do to acquire it. In doing this, the system flips on its head. Whereas before, the companies that were the most irresponsible made the most money, consumers can make it so that the most responsible companies make the most money. In the earlier example of the town bakery, what may happen in the future is that a bakery that only cares about profit doesn't get any sales, whereas a bakery that values the community and society as a whole is the one that consumers choose to shop at. Therefore, sort of paradoxically, for a firm to maximise profit, they will actually have to start caring about things other than profit. This consumer power is not to be taken lightly or to be underestimated by businesses. If exercised accordingly, it could quite quickly render this criticism of CSR as redundant.

With this in mind, there are several directions that this book could now go in, most noticeably splitting into the role that consumers need to play and the role that businesses need to play. While there is a little more to it than I've mentioned, the consumer's role is just a matter of buying stuff that comes from socially responsible companies, and a lot of data shows that more and more people are starting to do so. Therefore, the direction I'm going to go in surrounds what businesses will need to do to put themselves in a position where the new 'conscious consumers' will actively want to buy from them. To try and avoid some of the traps that have tripped up previous CSR academics, I like to think that the approach I'll propose throughout the remaining chapters will allow organisations to enjoy the benefits of 'successful' CSR in its purest and most effective form.

2

A Trinity of Sorts

By this point in the book, I like to think I've established the main ideas that justify everything else I'm going to talk about. It seems very clear that our ongoing relationship with money and desire for wealth have contributed to the philosophies that organisations traditionally adopt to determine success. As with the case of Apple, this continual striving for profit maximisation, while by no means inherently evil, has, until recently, created a system that rewards immorality. Companies that can get away with ruthless cost-cutting measures are the most profitable, and therefore 'successful' in the view of wider society. Fortunately, consumers are starting to realise their collective power and alter their purchasing decisions accordingly.

As a result, organisations that value social responsibility are starting to gain a competitive advantage. I'll drill down and discuss some of the data that I've collected in later chapters, but a 2015 Neilson study claimed that 66% of people were willing to pay more for socially/environmentally responsible products. This figure was a sizable increase from 55% in 2014 and 50% in 2013. They also noticed that opinions towards CSR were far more positive among younger age groups, highlighting to firms the potential future costs of ignoring the current millennial and generation Z demographics.

It therefore seems crucial that businesses adopt a CSR programme/strategy to make sure that when this new era of 'conscious consumers' becomes the norm, they have put themselves in a strong position to capitalise. It's at this point that the disparity between theory and practice becomes particularly prevalent. In essence, it's one thing to appreciate that your customers might want you to be socially responsible, it's another thing entirely to implement a strategy that reassures them that you actually are. I think that this is a problem that numerous businesses are currently facing, be it on a local or multinational scale. To maybe understand why, it's worthwhile reiterating the earlier criticism/misconception that CSR is just more and more things that businesses have to somehow juggle. This perception has created, and continues to create, CSR strategies that are fragmented and disjointed, which in turn results in quite an inefficient use of resources. What I mean by this, is that by viewing CSR as a long to-do list, companies end up engaging in the occasional random activity, which lacks the underlying sincerity that consumers are looking for. With this in mind, it's no wonder than CSR professionals have a hard time making the business case for all the work they're doing. If CSR isn't strategically thought out and implemented, the return on investment is likely to be quite low, if existent at all.

By this point, you may be thinking something along the lines of 'but surely CSR shouldn't be about return on investment, but making the world a better place?''. Funnily enough, this is where the second misconception from the previous chapter comes in, that CSR just takes away from a company's profit. This is also where we must address the issue of practicality. If businesses are going to take some of the responsibility for improving society, there will have to be something in it for them. Perhaps this is why people often dispute the effectiveness of CSR entirely. Companies that throw some resources at various altruistic projects might not see any visible value from doing so, and will, therefore, be disillusioned about its necessity. However, it is these companies that may be caught out in the future, when CSR and a corporate reputation of responsibility are increasingly important factors in consumer's purchasing decisions.

The main point I'm trying to make here is a simple one. Yes, some firms engage in CSR activities that are great for society, but they do so in a way that doesn't necessarily benefit them, meaning they tend not to keep them going. It should be noted that this is not an inherent issue with CSR as a concept. I genuinely believe, and I wouldn't be writing this book if I didn't, that, if implemented correctly, CSR could, and should, exist as a tool for businesses to both improve wider society and attract more of the customers of the future. I appreciate that this may sound like a bit of a 'win-win' situation, which usually all sound far too good to be true, but it's only as a result of existing misconceptions surrounding CSR that the idea sounds in any way abstract. However, for the sceptics among you, I'm hopefully going to use this chapter to prove that such a situation is perfectly attainable.

Before doing so, however, I think it's important to reflect, however briefly, on another underlying reason as to why such an approach is necessary. In comparison to other business disciplines (Marketing, Sales, HR etc.), CSR is pretty new. While academically it was being discussed in various books and journals in the mid 20th century, its practical application took a few decades to kick off. Even now, as I mentioned in the previous chapter, we're probably still only in its 'teenage years'. As a result, it's something organisations have started frantically adopting, which often means that the people responsible for managing CSR didn't know anything about it when they started in their position. This isn't a problem per se, as learning on the job is certainly achievable, but I think it would be unwise to rule out the possibility that CSR has suffered from a lack of education. As it's only just entering the education system, very few cohorts of individuals that have studied it have filtered into the necessary corporate positions.

A simple experiment using UCAS emphasises my point rather well. UCAS is the UK's central portal for higher education, and contains a feature where you can search for undergraduate courses. A search for a more common business function, in this case 'Marketing', returned 1393 options from various academic institutions. While I admit that studying at university is not the only way to learn and develop the necessary skills you need for a career; it certainly works as a proxy for showing how seriously it is taken when it comes to developing the next generation of professionals. In short, when looking at Marketing, educational institutions are equipping countless students with the necessary knowledge to influence organisational behaviour for generations to come. This knowledge will no doubt become the very expertise that will help make 'on the job' training and learning a simpler process.

A similar search for HR yielded 577 different courses, and the same logic can no doubt be applied. These business fields date back decades, and a system is in place to prepare and educate people accordingly. With this in mind, what do you think happened when I typed in CSR? Even to my surprise, I was greeted with 0 results, and a slightly patronising 'Did you mean car?'. The unabbreviated 'Corporate Social Responsibility' fared no better, with that search also coming back blank. I think this goes to show not just how quickly CSR as a concept has evolved, but also how it has 'crept up' on the traditional business world. It seems very much the case that consumers have grasped the idea far quicker than businesses, which in turn has caused them to act in a way that they perhaps wouldn't with other business functions. With CSR, there seems to be an element of trial and error, of making it up as you go along. How many businesses would adopt a similar approach to their marketing for example? Marketing is seen by many as more of an exact science, where following certain rules will help you maximise sales. CSR on the other hand, is perceived as a bit of an unknown quantity.

Despite this approach, the vast majority of firms have somehow managed to get away with it, potentially because no real CSR 'benchmark' exists for customers to compare against. As long are companies are trying to do something vaguely positive, consumers are willing to give them the benefit of the doubt. The margin for error is quite large. Fast forward to the near future, however, let's say ten years from now, and it may be a completely different story. CSR is already the fastest growing driver of corporate reputation, so it's a real possibility that it may influence corporate reputation just as easily as traditional marketing activity. If this does in fact become the case, the margin for error with CSR will surely narrow and become a far more fear-inducing prospect for firms to try and negotiate.

It's probably worth admitting at this point that I don't exactly consider myself to be an 'expert' in this field. To be perfectly honest, I'd be tempted to question whether or not the title of 'expert' can even be awarded. CSR is undergoing a sustained period of academic discovery. New ideas are being proposed all the time, and this book is a mere example of that. I don't think there will ever be a point where somebody can claim a complete understanding of it, simply because the business world is constantly going to change and evolve. What that makes me, therefore, is a rather enthusiastic 'learner' within the field of CSR. A learner who can combine research, logic and experience of working in the field to generate some form of insight. Although obviously biased, I can't help but think such an approach could be useful. As a concept, CSR has been quite heavily monopolised by academics, which in turn has diluted any meaningful sense of pragmatism. Similarly, it's also been quite consistently over-intellectualised, leaving businesses at a bit of a loose end when it comes to devising any form of strategy. In short, there aren't the same types of basic applicable concepts that exist in other business areas. That is partly what I hope to change. However ambitious or naïve, I think it's possible to present CSR in a logical and straightforward manner, a manner that can actually be useful for interested organisations.

So how can I go about doing this? Reluctantly, the old cliché about needing solid foundations before you can build anything long lasting is quite relevant here. In the same way that a tree requires a network of roots to promote its growth and success, CSR needs some underlying mechanism from which everything else can be derived. From all my research and work within the field of CSR, I think it's possible to present the foundations of it as three basic criteria. That is to say that if a CSR strategy follows three basic principles, its likelihood of success (for both society and the business) will be maximised. For the visual learners among you, the following diagram is a representation of this concept, which hopefully clarifies what I'm talking about.

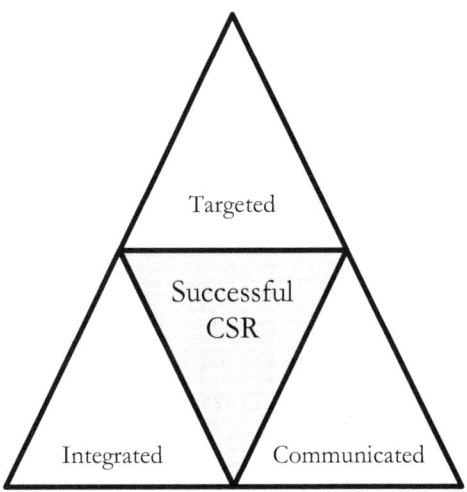

The general idea is that the three outside triangles represent the necessary criteria for CSR to be effective. Consider it to be a 'trinity' of sorts. The centre triangle (in this case 'successful CSR') can only exist when the three outside triangles are combined.

As this implies, no one particular criterion is more important than any other. Some may give the illusion of heightened importance, but there isn't one of the three principles that could be removed without the chances of success sharply diminishing.

To give a comprehensive explanation of these concepts in a way that is both theoretically justifiable and practically useful, the next three chapters will each focus on one of the outer triangles. The remainder of this chapter, therefore, will serve as a form of introduction, establishing a base level of understanding that will increase the effectiveness of the rest of the book.

The first thing to touch on is the centre triangle, as we need to acknowledge the difficulties associated with the term 'successful CSR'. Having worked in CSR, I can comfortably say that one of the biggest challenges to overcome is that it's really difficult to measure the success of it. When working within a more recognised department, Sales, for instance, the unit of measurement is so overwhelmingly obvious that it doesn't require a second thought. With something like CSR, that doesn't necessarily exist. Is 'success' measured by how much money a firm gives to charity? By how many volunteer hours its staff give up for charitable causes? Maybe it can be measured by the number of trees they plant or the amount of plastic they recycle? The truth is that none of these metrics will bring you anywhere closer to confidently saying whether or not a CSR programme has been successful. After all, while some quantifiable acts of benevolence exist, the majority of factors can't be quantified, working conditions being a prime example.

To try and overcome this issue of measuring success, we must start off by imaging what it might look like. Going back to what I mentioned earlier, and what motivated me to create such a framework is the idea that when companies implement CSR effectively, it should benefit both society and the business in question. This balance is only possible as a result of consumers actively seeking out responsible companies, but, providing they continue to do so, it's a balance that is certainly achievable from a corporate perspective. Success in this instance therefore simply means achieving this balance. I think this is a better definition of success because it incorporates the notion that for CSR to be successful, it has to be sustainable. When I say sustainable it's worth noting that I'm not referring to any form of environmental preservation usually associated with the word, rather the literal definition of being able to carry on doing something. If CSR benefits an organisation in some way or another, they are far more likely to keep doing it, and if they're helping society at the same time, then everybody wins.

However, as I've mentioned, defining success is merely solving the first part of a two-part problem. We may know what success means, but can we ever measure it? If Primark suddenly improve the working conditions of all their global suppliers and communicate it effectively, they may increase some sales. However, how can they ever be genuinely sure as to which sales have come as a direct result of their CSR activity? Sure, you might be able to track some general level of positivity on social media platforms or get some qualitative feedback from customer surveys, but in reality, you'll struggle to find anything conclusive.

Personally, I don't see this as the sort of monumental issue that many others view it as. Having worked in the UK subsidiary of a global organisation, I'm only too familiar with the constant need to measure the success of every action and project. It's almost as if everything needs at least three key performance indicators before you should even bother doing it. In all seriousness though, I completely get the reasoning behind measuring everything. Businesses need to know if what they're doing is worth doing again, or whether they need to change things up and approach a problem differently. When it comes to CSR, I think it requires a slightly different outlook. Going back to the idea of striking a balance between business and societal benefit, I think as long as a firm's CSR activity has some positive effect on society without leaving them unable to continue doing it, then it must be viewed as successful. In many ways, that's the only real measurement that matters. We may be able to track the odd metric here and there, or utilise some third party accreditations, but suggesting that some form of universal performance indicator exists won't provide us with any meaningful insight.

Building on this idea of longevity and sustainability, it would appear, to some extent at least, that a firm's scope for any form of positive social influence is confined by the parameters of what can be maintained over a prolonged period. For example, a small local company with not many resources has a drastically different capacity for CSR than a multinational company with seemingly limitless resources. If the local company tries to match the activities of the larger organisation, they'll probably go bankrupt pretty quickly. If the larger organisation only invests the resources of the small organisation, the social benefit in relation to their size would be laughable. Therefore, what both companies face is the challenge of finding a sustainable way of maximising both the social and organisational benefits generated from the respective resources at their disposal. That is what the above framework aims to do. Each of the three criteria, if met, will allow a business to gain a competitive advantage from their activities, all while helping society at the same time. With that being said, we can now briefly introduce each of the three criteria, and the form that meeting them may take in a business context. While none of them are any more important than any other, there is a logical order that it makes sense to discuss them in, the first of which starts right at the top.

Targeted

The concept of targeted CSR is a crucial one and one that makes sense as the starting block for any interested organisation. Briefly put, this criterion addresses the fragmented nature of CSR that I've already spoken about. For many companies, CSR is more of a culmination of a wide range of individual projects and activities, rather than a strategic discipline in which everything is in some way connected. In the next chapter, where the idea of targeted CSR will be discussed in far more detail, I'll offer up a matrix that enables organisations to categorise their activities. It's only by breaking down their behaviour in this way that businesses can understand how certain activities are effecting their commercial success. In doing this, a company is just one step away from being able to focus more specifically on the initiatives which add the most value, while holding back slightly on the ones with minimal benefits. Think of it in some way similar to the 'jack of all trades, master of none' philosophy. With CSR, it's probably better to focus on some key issues and have a greater impact, than spread yourself too thin and barely make any progress on any individual project. The truth is, certain CSR activities will be a far more effective use of resources than others, and being able to identify where they all fit can be an extremely valuable exercise.

Throughout this book, I've tended to adopt a mixture of hypothetical and real-life examples to emphasise my points. As I move away from theory and into the more complex world of practical implementation, I try to use as many real-life examples as possible. This will help show actual instances where following these criteria, albeit without companies recognising that they are doing so, has led to the ongoing 'success' that we have recently discussed. Looking at the idea of 'targeted' CSR, a great example would be a company like Kenco coffee. For a number of years now, Kenco have been working on what they call their 'Coffee Vs Gangs' initiative. Kenco were able to acknowledge that the countries where they grew their coffee had extremely high crime rates, with young people often turning to a life of gangs and crime as a result of the distinct lack of other opportunities. What Kenco then decided to do was create a whole education program, offering meaningful employment prospects to the individuals within these countries. Because this initiative directly linked to their business, and these workers were stakeholders of the company (going back to that theory), it made perfect sense for Kenco to consider themselves responsible for their welfare. Fast forward a few years, and the Coffee Vs Gangs campaign is viewed very positively amongst consumers and has helped alter their corporate reputation for the better. It is the process of identifying these types of activities that I will look at in the next chapter.

Integrated

After understanding the effects of different types of CSR activities, the logical 'next step', if you like, will be to look at how a business can take the issues they are planning to focus on and use them to strengthen their corporate reputation. One of the main concepts that will be discussed here relates to the subtle yet fundamental difference between doing responsible things and doing things responsibly. As you may have guessed, being known as a responsible company is far better than being seen a company that has done a few responsible things. However, when it comes to CSR, numerous companies seem to stop at the previous step of targeting.

While it's obviously important for an organisation to select the issues that matter to them successfully, it's just as essential that they spend time incorporating them into the identity of their business. Fortunately, there are still endless examples of firms successfully meeting this criterion, with previously mentioned companies like The Body Shop and Ben and Jerry's instantly coming to mind. The issues that matter to both of these organisations are so deeply ingrained that to some extent they can't be easily separated as distinct activities or initiatives. When it comes to integration, the real discussion here involves quite a philosophical debate around consequentialism. It may seem slightly unrelated, but it can be discussed by trying to answer the question of what is more beneficial, companies that strive to 'give something back' or companies that don't 'take' in the first place?

That is what we mean when we talk about integration. It's about taking the issues identified in the first stage and incorporating them so profoundly, that all commercial behaviour has a CSR component.

It's only really when an organisation has successfully met this criterion that it can move onto the third and final part of the framework. It's by no means a quick and easy task, but again by looking at examples of companies that have managed it, and also companies that haven't, the positive effects of trying will hopefully become apparent.

Communicated

Quite comfortably the most underrated and underappreciated component of CSR is communication. I've mentioned several times throughout this book that the only thing making 'successful' CSR possible is the fact that a new era of conscious consumers is demanding socially responsible goods from socially responsible companies. With that in mind, it seems quite reasonable to assume that effectively communicating with them is pivotal to gaining their trust as buyers. As consumers start to look for responsible companies, firms must become a beacon of benevolence, helping buyers understand all the great work they're doing. Without this crucial step, the whole idea of using CSR to gain competitive advantage becomes obsolete.

I can completely understand why many people misunderstand the communication element of CSR. On the one hand, businesses want to tell customers how great they are, but at the same time, they don't want customers to see it all as a big PR opportunity. Sincerity plays a sizable role here. There are few things worse than a company that continually overhypes how socially responsible they are just to desperately try and attract that one extra sale. Consumers are starting to see through that.

As a result, there are some communication methods that are reliably more successful than others. This is a prime example of where the three criteria overlap. If the CSR initiatives are appropriately targeted, they will naturally appeal to potential customers of that product and communication will be easier to manage. Likewise, integration is also essential, as it's far more believable for a company to communicate what sort of company they are, rather than what sort of things they have done. As I've said, it's quite a subtle difference, but a significant one nonetheless.

So there you have it. That's pretty much a whistle-stop tour of the next three chapters. Of course, what I aim to do as we move forward is combine the logic of the framework with more detailed real-life examples. I'll also introduce and discuss the results of the research I have conducted that helped me create it in the first place.

What I hope these ideas start to do is present CSR in a way that becomes a bit more tangible to an extent. It's so easy and tempting for companies to continue seeing CSR as an abstract concept where as long as a they're doing something vaguely beneficial, then all is good. I think that such an approach could be damaging over the next couple of decades. In the businesses of the future, CSR needs to be held to the same standard and viewed with the same credibility and importance as other business areas. If CSR is going to one day be as common as the idea of Marketing or HR, then it will surely be an oversight to consider it as something of limited importance. By viewing and respecting it as a legitimate business practice, companies will be able to get the most out of it.

That's why it's necessary to try and maximise resource efficiency, maximise social and organisational benefits, and understand what needs to be done in order to do so. It's only when businesses view CSR as something that's both advantageous to them and simple to implement, that they will ever adopt it on a scale broad enough to make any noticeable difference.

3

Busy Bandwagons

This chapter marks the start of drawing on some real-life research to strengthen the concept of targeted CSR that I've already touched upon. With most companies adopting a very fragmented approach, this chapter will explicitly highlight the critical role that targeting can play when it comes to both organisational and societal 'success'. It's worth reiterating at this point that all of these ideas and concepts rely on the assumption, albeit a justifiable one, that consumers are starting to look at CSR when making purchasing decisions. The idea that this behaviour will become more common amongst consumers is still at the heart of what makes CSR so important, and the concepts outlined in this book may enable businesses to begin to capitalise on such a trend.

I'll start off by highlighting what I set out to achieve when I started conducting this research. With more and more examples of CSR slowly entering the mainstream business world, I found myself observing what I could only explain as a subtle but significant difference between the various types of socially responsible activities. The word 'activity' in this instance may not be the best way to view it, but I use it as a word to describe any responsible behaviour or action that a company has undertaken. The difference I noticed was prompted by observing how my perception of a company (in terms of their level of responsibility) varied depending on what sort of issues they were pledging to tackle or even eradicate. I couldn't help but think that when Velvet, a UK toilet paper company, said they'd plant three trees for every one they use, it meant more to me than when Leesa, a fast-growing mattress company, promised to plant one tree for each sale. I don't think this was just because planting three trees is better than planting one. Given the nature of their products, it just felt more appropriate for Velvet to invest in tackling deforestation. After all, trees provide Velvet with the primary raw material that they need for creating their toilet paper in the first place. Don't get me wrong, Leesa are by no means being irresponsible or insincere with their pledge, it just felt less purposeful when it came to influencing my perception of them. After all, consumers perceiving a company as responsible is the only way that companies can achieve organisational success and societal success simultaneously. With this in mind, I set out to devise a consumer study that could maybe determine whether or not I was onto something.

This project quickly led me to one of my main frustrations with CSR from an academic perspective. Before setting out on my quest for consumer feedback, I wanted to try and see if anybody had carried out a similar study. However, all I found were endless studies (most of which were largely similar) that merely demonstrated that consumers care about CSR and will pay more for it. That conclusion is all well and good, and, as I've mentioned, underpins this whole book, but it isn't particularly useful when it comes to exploring CSR further. Broadly speaking, very few bits of research manage to reach a conclusion that organisations can practically implement, other than telling them that CSR is worthwhile. What we're effectively doing is moaning at businesses to do something, but without giving them any meaningful guidance for going about it efficiently. If we want to start to utilise and harness the power that organisations have with regards to making the world a better place, it seems only fair that we give them a bit more to work with. We want them to clean our house, but we're just giving them a toothbrush. It's no wonder they're not doing the best job.

For some reason or another I was quite optimistic about the research I was planning to conduct. I knew it would have to somehow track and measure how consumers perceive companies as a result of behaving in specific ways, but that concept felt quite achievable. Most CSR research (including some of my own that I'll mention in a later chapter), is about purchasing behaviour. The underlying implication with that is that it's one thing for consumers to say they'll spend more on a responsible product, it's an entirely different thing to actually do it. As a result, any research about purchasing intent, unless combined with actual purchasing patterns, needs to be taken with a pinch of salt. Studying perception, however, has a far less significant disparity between theory and practice. If under hypothetical circumstances, somebody perceives a company to be responsible, that perception is unlikely to wildly change if such a situation then occurred in real life. Still, I knew that I had to put some thought into the way I conducted my research. Having already admitted that the difference between my perceptions of companies is often subtle, I needed a way to position the logic within more extreme scenarios to see if I could establish a general rule.

The study worked like so. I started off by creating two simple questions. In each question, respondents were told about two hypothetical companies of the same size/revenue, which had recently acted in the same responsible way. The only difference between the two companies was the industry in which they operated. With only the information available to them, the respondents just had to select whether they thought one company was more responsible than the other (and if so, which one) or whether they thought they were both the same. The reason I used two questions instead of just one was simply to gain even more data to see if I could identify a common trend. The first question involved a hypothetical Wood Furniture Company and a Bakery, while the second featured an Automotive Company and a Social Media Site. These generic terms were exactly how the companies were presented to the respondents, so no pre-existing views of particular brands or organisations could influence their answers. There was, however, a critical feature of each of these questions. For question one, the CSR activity that both the Wood Furniture Company and the Bakery had carried out was the planting of 1000 trees. For question two, the CSR activity surrounded the responsible use of customer's data.

As you have probably noticed, within each of the questions, the CSR activity is far more applicable to one of the two hypothetical businesses. Planting trees is a naturally more relevant action for a Wood Furniture Company, while data protection is probably more relevant to a Social Media Site than the Automotive Company. Going back to my own experience, I wanted to see if, like me, people would view the Wood Furniture Company as more responsible than the Bakery, and likewise with the Social Media site. I figured that such a result would go some way to proving some of the ideas I have about why targeted CSR is essential. However, it was also vital to include the option for people to say that both companies were equally responsible. Especially for consumers that don't particularly value CSR, it would make complete sense to simply argue that if two companies do the same activity, then they are just as responsible as each other.

So what were the results of this study? Well, firstly, I was able to note that of the people surveyed, 67% of them implied that industry context affected perception in some way. That is to say that these people viewed one company as more responsible than the other in at least one of the questions. Considering that the only variable between the two companies in each question was the type of company they were, it seems reasonable to assume that it was the main, if not sole, factor in people's perceptions of their responsibility. With regards to my hypothesis, it was very much a case of 'so far, so good' at this point, but the real test of my theory was yet to be demonstrated conclusively. That being said, the next conclusion I was able to draw from the data was of enormous importance. I wanted to look at the results of just those who said that one company was more responsible than the other, obviously seeing if they chose the company that I thought they would. The results of that particular bit of analysis for question one can be seen below:

Of the people that said one company was more responsible:	
Wood Furniture Company	81%
Bakery	19%

As you can quite clearly see, of the people that didn't think the companies were equally responsible, they overwhelmingly selected the Wood Furniture Company. Remember of course, that the CSR activity in this question was planting trees, something which I would argue is far more appropriate for a Wood Furniture Company to engage in than a Bakery. However, this was just the first question, and to try and add some credibility to my point, I'd need to look at the results of the second question too. Remember that for this question, the choice was between an Automotive Company and a Social Media site, with the CSR activity being responsible data protection. Considering the amount of data we, often unknowingly, give to Social Media sites, for my hypothesis to stand any chance of being justified, consumers would have to see the Social Media site as being more responsible than the Automotive Company. In similar fashion to question one, I looked at the responses from the consumers who perceived one company to be more responsible than the other. These were the results:

Of the people that said one company was more responsible:	
Automotive Company	11%
Social Media Site	89%

In this question, the company for which the CSR behaviour was more 'applicable' received an even larger share of the answers. In combination with the results of the first question, the notion that perhaps public perception was not simply decided based on CSR activity, but on the context within which that activity sits, was slowly coming together.

It is, however, worthwhile addressing the argument that people could make in favour of the Bakery and the Automotive

Company in these questions. While I'm saying that companies are most responsible when they tackle issues more applicable to their industry, you could say, for example, that the Bakery is more responsible because, in planting trees, they are doing something that they aren't necessarily obligated to do. Similarly, you could say that the Social Media Site are more obliged to protect data, so it's actually more admirable for the Automotive Company to pledge to do so. While there is logic to this opinion, I think it perhaps misses the bigger picture of CSR. Just think, if a company *only* engages in one CSR activity, which is exactly what these questions were suggesting, surely it is more important for the Wood Furniture Company to plant the trees? This is the main point that encouraged me to carry out this research in the first place. After all, companies have limited resources that they will dedicate to social responsibility, so it's very important that they work out where they will best be utilised. That's not to say that companies should plough them all into addressing one specific issue, but they should have a few industry relevant ones that they prioritise, before choosing to tackle anything else. The data from the two above tables goes some way to proving this point, demonstrating that CSR should be a strategic business practice.

Before we get too ahead of ourselves, however, we shouldn't forget about the 33% of people that viewed both companies as equally responsible. After all, the two companies have equal resources and were behaving in exactly the same way, so such a viewpoint does make sense. In many ways, it was actually quite surprising that the number of people who adopted this opinion was as high as 67%.

Anyway, as I've already mentioned, CSR is still in a growth phase, and consumers aren't all completely on-board with it. As a result, there is bound to be a certain degree of apathy amongst those consumers who aren't particularly convinced about its importance. I would guess, and it may very well be the subject of future research, that as recognition for CSR continues to grow, the number of people that see context as a relevant factor will increase. After all, as more and more companies start adopting CSR practices, there will need to be useful ways of differentiating them from one another. Relating their behaviour to the adverse societal effects of their industry may be a viable method of doing just that.

However, before getting too carried away, there was more research to be conducted to genuinely concrete my views on CSR. For all I knew, there existed a really abstract predisposition that meant people would always view Social Media Sites and Wood Furniture Companies as pioneers of social responsibility. I highly doubted that of course, but I didn't think it would hurt to dig a bit deeper to prove it. To do so, I carried out a second round of the study. In this round, I used precisely the same two questions, with exactly the same two companies. The only change I made was to make sure that this time, the CSR behaviour in each question was more positively geared towards the other company. For the first question, therefore, I stated that both companies had decided to provide food to the homeless.

With one company being a Bakery, this was naturally more applicable to them than the Wood Furniture Store (unlike the planting trees behaviour from the first round). After all, food waste is a monumental issue at the moment, and many shops that sell food are being publically encouraged to do something valuable with it instead of merely throwing away everything they don't sell at the end of the day. The issue has resonated so profoundly with the public that in December 2017, Tesco announced that 'no food fit for human consumption' would go to waste. In an initiative that is set to involve all 2,654 stores across the UK, unsold food will be donated to shelters, food banks and other charitable organisations.

For the second question, I changed the CSR behaviour to 'CO$_2$ Neutrality'. CO$_2$ Neutrality is the practice of a company reducing and offsetting their CO$_2$ emissions so that their net emissions are effectively zero. Naturally, this would be far more of an applicable pledge for the Automotive Company to make than the Social Media site. What I would have therefore expected was for the respondents to, this time around, view the Bakery and the Automotive Company as more responsible. This would rule out the idea that people had some sort of natural preference towards Wood Furniture Companies and Social Media Sites and increase the likelihood that the factor influencing their decision was, in fact, the contextual relevance of the CSR activities in question.

Before looking at each question, I wanted to see the number of people who that thought context mattered at all, the people that didn't simply believe that both companies were the equally responsible in both questions. This round of the study used a brand new set of consumers, so it was interesting to note that among this group, 66% thought context played a part in some way. As this result is incredibly similar to the 67% recorded from the first part of the study, it reinforces the earlier conclusion that roughly 30-35% of people judge CSR purely based on the actions of a business, without looking at the context. It's also important to note that while this round of the study used a new set of consumers, their gender and age was randomised and, as a result of the sample size, statistically similar to the previous group.

For the first question this time around, again just focussing on the answers from those who decided that one business was more responsible than the other, the results were as follows:

Of the people that said one company was more responsible:	
Wood Furniture Company	27%
Bakery	73%

While the margin of victory, so to speak, was lower for the Bakery in this round than it was for the Wood Furniture Company in the first round, it's still quite conclusive. When the CSR activity was more applicable to the Wood Furniture Company, consumers perceived them as more responsible. When the CSR activity was geared towards the Bakery, the opposite occurred. To confirm this view, it's also worth looking at the results of the second question, which can be seen below:

Of the people that said one company was more responsible:	
Automotive Company	90%
Social Media Site	10%

With this question, I was able to record the biggest 'win' for a company out of the entire study. I imagine that because emissions are so relevant to the automotive industry as a whole, a company that pledges to make their net emissions effectively zero will no doubt benefit over companies in other industries. The interesting point here, however, is that IT-intensive companies, a sector to which all Social Media Sites obviously belong, produce more than their fair share of emissions too. The amount of electricity required to maintain their endless computer equipment and all the servers they rely on is hardly a drop in the ocean.

However, what this goes to show is that consumers have very clear views about what social problems certain businesses should set out to try and solve. Almost regardless of how much CO_2 a Social Media Site produces, it will probably always be more of a concern with Automotive Companies. Likewise, no matter how much data Automotive Companies collect, consumers will react better when Social Media Sites pledge to use it responsibly. If companies can identify the issues that matter the most to their target market, they will be better poised to generate a return on investment from their activities. I'll come back to this in more detail later, but first, its necessary to look at the third and final round of my consumer study.

By this point, I was quite confident that an organisation using CSR to tackle the issues that related most heavily to their industry positively maximised the public's view of them. The final thing I needed to do, however, was investigate how CSR behaviours were perceived when they weren't in any way industry specific. What about something like tax avoidance? Or equal pay for men and women? Sure, some industries have particularly poor reputations for these matters, but there aren't industries for which paying the fair amount of tax is more applicable than others. As consumers, these are the kind of behaviours that we would like all businesses to adopt, irrespective of the context. I wanted to explore this a bit further, so repeated the study with another new set of respondents, this time with the CSR activity in each question being no more relevant to one of the companies than the other. For the first question, I looked at tax avoidance, claiming that neither companies engaged in any type of avoidance scheme. For the second question, I looked at the gender pay gap, stating that both companies ensured that male and female staff were paid equally. The results for each question can be seen on the following page:

For the first question:

When asked which company was the most responsible:	
Wood Furniture Company	11%
Bakery	5%
Both Equal	84%

And for the second question:

When asked which company was the most responsible:	
Automotive Company	8%
Social Media Site	11%
Both Equal	81%

In this instance, when the CSR activity was more generic, neither company came out on top as being any more socially responsible than the other. For both questions, the most common answer was that both firms were equally responsible. After completing this final round, I finally felt comfortable in confirming that my original view of CSR was correct. In essence, we can separate CSR into two different forms of activity. On the one hand, we have generic activity, which isn't in any way specific to any particular industry. On the other hand, we have targeted activity. Targeted activity is an activity that directly relates to the key societal issues associated with the industry that a business operates in. It's important to note that I am not suggesting that either generic or targeted activities are better than the other. What I will do, however, is indicate that both types of activity have a different purpose and role within the broader concept of CSR. For now, these two activity types will simply form the first part of a CSR matrix, a matrix which we can later use to understand the effect that different activities can have on organisations. So far, we have something that looks a little bit like this:

Generic	Targeted	?
		?

What we therefore need to do is fill in the blanks. Upon knowing that CSR activities are either generic or targeted, the words that will soon replace the two question marks can be logically derived. From the research I conducted, it was quite clear that if a company within one industry engaged in some targeted activity, their reputation amongst the public would generally be better than if a company from another sector did the same thing. That's useful to know to an extent, but it's hardly reassuring for businesses. First and foremost, companies don't tend to compete with companies from other industries. A wood furniture company won't ever compete with a bakery, so why would it matter if their reputation for CSR is better than theirs? What the wood furniture company would be interested in, is ensuring that their reputation for CSR is better than all the other wood furniture companies.

At this point we must ask ourselves the question, how would consumer perception differ between two companies in the same industry engaging in the same activity? On the face of it, it wouldn't. If the industry was the only thing making consumers choose one company over another in my study, then removing that variable would no doubt remove any sense of preference towards a particular business. In real life, however, that assumption doesn't necessarily hold. Both M&S and Primark both claim that they do their best to maximise working conditions for people in their factories and that no child labour is used, but who do you have a higher opinion of? M&S I assume. Now, that may be because M&S products are more expensive than Primark's, so it's more believable that they've actually dedicated some resources to better working conditions, but what about similarly priced companies. What if we looked at M&S and Debenhams? Why is it that M&S have won countless awards for responsibility whereas Debenhams haven't? Clearly, there is another component in play here.

This component, however, is a bit less black and white that the 'Generic' and 'Targeted' options that we have already established. However, I believe it's still possible to broadly categorise it into two separate labels. The labels I think suit it most accurately are 'Proactive' and 'Reactive', and hopefully, the reason for such categorisation will become clear as we work towards completing the matrix I introduced on the previous page. For starters, the reason I like the words proactive and reactive is because they are multifaceted to an extent. Proactive often means that you are first to do something, but it also means, in this context at least, that you are taking it seriously and acting with a degree of sincerity. These two meanings go hand it hand pretty well. If you take an issue really seriously, you're likely to try and tackle it before other people do. Conversely, the word 'reactive' suggests that exact opposite. Perhaps as a result of not taking an issue particularly seriously, reactive CSR is essentially the phrase we can use for when companies jump on the bandwagon of something that competitors have been focusing on for ages.

The more we look at real-life examples, the more we can start to segregate different CSR strategies into these two categories. Going back to the case of clothing, M&S launched their CSR initiative known as 'Plan A' all the way back in 2007, and they're constantly evolving it to include new targets and ambitions that they hope to achieve. It would be a fair assessment to view M&S as proactive in this instance. Primark on the other hand only parted with factories that used child labour in response to a BBC Panorama programme in 2008, not necessarily as a result of their own ethical stance. 5 years later, one of their factories in Dhaka, Bangladesh, collapsed, killing 1,134 people. In response, Primark paid out millions in compensation, but a proactive firm would have arguably prevented such a tragedy in the first place.

To be honest, Primark's actions probably don't even count as 'reactive CSR' because, by definition, reactive CSR still has to actually be CSR. You could argue that Primark doesn't even do enough to fit into the 'reactive' category, but I'll touch on that in more detail a bit later on. Generally speaking though, companies can either be proactive in tackling issues, or they can hurriedly jump on the bandwagon when all hell breaks loose. Perhaps the sad reality when looking at CSR in this way is that while there are some exceptional examples of firms leading the way, there are also a fair few busy bandwagons out there, gradually filling up as companies rush to save their reputation.

With this component of CSR now established, we can complete the matrix that I think adequately explains the various forms that CSR can take, and how it can harm or benefit the business in question. By adding the 'Proactive' and 'Reactive' labels, and then by deriving the consequences of each combination, we end up with a matrix that looks this:

Activity Scope

Generic	Targeted		
Risk Mitigation	Competitive Advantage	*Proactive*	**Company Approach**
Risk-Taking	Reputational Apathy	*Reactive*	

For the remainder of the chapter, I'll look at each of the four centre quadrants and explain what I mean by the name I have decided to give them. I should probably mention that despite the four distinct areas, it shouldn't be the case that an organisation solely sits in one of them. In an ideal world, companies should be proactive for both targeted issues and generic ones.

Where the matrix comes in handy, is for enabling organisations to visualise how their resources are being used, identify what benefits or consequences their activities are bringing them, and decide whether or not they need to increase their investment. Still, I'll come back to that a bit later, but for now, I'll start by looking at the part that probably sounds the most appealing from a business perspective, which is naturally 'Competitive Advantage'.

Competitive Advantage

As the matrix depicts, using CSR to achieve a competitive advantage requires an organisation to combine specific, targeted issues with a proactive company approach. You'll be able to notice from the matrix that this is the only combination that results in a competitive advantage. To understand why this is, there is quite a logical thought process which can be followed. As I highlighted when introducing the idea of Generic and Targeted activities, the research showed that companies in an industry that relates more closely to a given issue (e.g. automotive industry and the issue of emissions), will enjoy a greater benefit regarding reputation than companies in other sectors. We must understand that this fundamentally means that, using the example of emissions, an automotive company has a comparative advantage over a social media company, for example. Notice the difference between a *comparative* advantage and a *competitive* advantage.

A comparative advantage in this instance simply means that relative to the social media site, the automotive company is in a better position to tackle the issue of emissions and gain reputational benefits as a result. Going back to the research I conducted, if an automotive company has a comparative advantage with emissions, then a social media company has a comparative advantage over the automotive company when it comes to data protection. This is not to say that any one company will be more effective in tackling either of the two issues. The automotive company may have the resources to make data protection their key social aim, but the return on the investment of those resources will be lower than that of the social media company. Basically, comparative advantage is just a fancy way of saying companies should focus on what they'll benefit the most from.

So, if this gives firms a comparative advantage, how does it become a competitive advantage? Well, that's where proactivity comes in. Assuming that an automotive company has now realised how important reducing emissions is, they are now in competition with all the other automotive companies that have recognised the same thing. From now on, success will be less about the issue they are tackling, and more about how they're addressing it. If a firm takes a proactive approach, pledging to lead the way when it comes to reducing emissions and innovating new methods of getting around that are entirely sustainable, then they're going to come out on top when consumers choose who to by from. It's only by being proactive that consumers will know just how seriously businesses are taking it, and, unless rivals are miraculously efficient, it will also increase the chances of a firm making noticeable progress before anybody else. To put a name to the automotive example I've been using, maybe a company like Toyota would fit the bill. The environment, including emissions, is Toyota's primary focus of their CSR strategy, and they're leading the market with concepts like hybrid cars and now even hydrogen vehicles. Another example might be a company like The Body Shop. The Body Shop focused on an issue that was extremely relevant to the cosmetics industry, and started doing something about it before anybody else even considered it. Now their entire reputation surrounds their ethics and social responsibility.

The final thing I would say on competitive advantage, and particularly on taking a proactive approach, is that it's currently not too late to start. Even if a company is way further behind than some competitors, they can probably still decide to become proactive about an issue and invest in it accordingly. If they keep at it and the front runners get complacent, competitive advantage is there for the taking. However, this window of opportunity may not last for long, and companies that haven't started addressing their key social issues in several years' time may not be able to recover. It's also worth stating that competitive advantage is, of course, all relative. A company like Nissan can have a CSR advantage over a company like Kia, without having an advantage over Toyota. Generally speaking, it's only by continuing to adopt a reactive approach that a company will remain desperately clutching onto the bandwagon.

Reputational Apathy

Speaking of continuing to adopt a reactive approach, it makes sense to talk about reputational apathy. Reputational apathy is the best phrase I could think of that actively describes how reactive CSR influences consumers. Notice that I use the word 'apathy' instead of something far more negative like 'damage'. It's important to highlight that this matrix is only applicable to types of CSR activity, as opposed to CSR inactivity, so for a company to sit somewhere on the matrix they still have to be involved in some sort of CSR initiative. That's why I think reputational apathy is a fitting description, and a company like Debenhams might be a good example of it. By nature, they're doing more than companies like Primark, but they're nowhere near the level of M&S. When I think about Debenhams' reputation as a responsible business, I'm not immediately swayed in either direction. They're not, to my knowledge anyway, so unethical that I'd never buy from them again, but if I were looking for a responsible clothing company, they wouldn't come to mind.

If I were to speculate for a moment, I would guess that the vast majority of businesses, especially ones in the public eye, sit in this quadrant. They'll try and do what they can to make sure people don't view them as irresponsible, but there's currently no incentive to go any further just yet. In the short term, of course, they may be correct, but as consumers start to value CSR more and more, that approach will no doubt need to change.

Risk Mitigation

The third quadrant I'd like to look at is risk mitigation, as you may wonder why proactively approaching a generic issue is worth such an understated label. To understand this, it's worth reflecting back on the sorts of generic activities that will fall under this category. When we looked at targeted activities, we noticed that they were usually activities that directly aimed to negate the negative social consequences of a particular industry. Cars create emissions, so emissions reduction is a targeted activity for a car company. Generic activities though don't have such a straightforward derivation. When we think of examples of generic activities, they are usually things that we as consumers just expect organisations to engage in. Paying the fair amount of tax, not discriminating when employing people, paying men and women fairly etc. These are all perfect examples of generic activities.

The interesting point to notice, however, is that with generic activities, consumers will react negatively if a business doesn't do them, but won't act positively if they do. I'm not going to start shopping at a particular clothing store if they pay their taxes, but I might stop shopping with them if they don't. Realistically, being proactive about generic activities such as eradicating a gender pay gap or paying corporation tax isn't even newsworthy. I'd be able to give you an example of companies that don't pay their tax, but when it comes to companies that do, I'd have to assume it's just everybody else unless I learn otherwise.

What this entire concept does is inject an element of risk management into CSR. These types of activities may not bolster a firm's reputation, but they can prevent it from suddenly hitting rock bottom when an investigative journalist exposes them for unethical business practices. Therefore, the combination of generic activities with a proactive approach is a means of mitigating that risk, which in itself can be extremely worthwhile for a company's reputation.

Risk-Taking

Conversely, it should now be quite easy to understand why a reactive approach to generic activities could be seen as risk-taking. If a company steadily plods along doing the bare minimum that keeps them out of trouble, they open themselves up to one day being exposed for how far behind other companies they are. Some companies may consider this risk worthwhile if the short-term financial gain outweighs the long-term economic consequences of reputational damage, but that's for those in charge to decide. Naturally, I would argue that this sort of approach shouldn't be adopted if it can be avoided in any way. I like to think of it like sneaking on a train without a train ticket. If your train ticket costs a fiver and the penalty for being caught without one is £20, then you've only got to get away with it 4 times for it to be worth it. While harder to speculate, I would imagine many companies are taking this sort of approach, especially with issues such as tax avoidance and the gender pay gap.

The issue is, from the company's perspective, that the candle is being burnt at both ends, so to speak. On the one hand, people are becoming more persistent at exposing the irresponsible ways in which companies operate, while on the other hand, the reputation damage will gradually increase. It's the equivalent of more ticket inspectors and raising the fine to £50. Taking the risk suddenly becomes a far less desirable proposition.

So, with each of the four quadrants explained, how can the matrix actually benefit organisations in any way? Well, for starters, I would suggest that most companies could benefit from using it to identify where their resources are being used. If they're using all of their resources on *proactive* generic activity, then they'll probably only be leaving enough for *reactive* targeted activity, and that may be cause for concern. Similarly, if a firm decided to throw all their resources at a proactive targeted activity, then it would naturally leave very few resources for the generic activities, running the risk of potentially damaging their reputation in the long run. I guess that an important thing to reiterate is the idea that companies shouldn't just sit in one of these four quadrants.

The primary function of this matrix is, therefore, to help businesses find some form of balance. By understanding where all of their activities sit, they should be able to combine what would be an otherwise fragmented CSR strategy, resulting in the inefficient use of resources.

What it can also be used to do is highlight the problem of activities that are not explicitly targeted to a company's industry, but also not universal across all industries. As the matrix suggests, such an activity would fail to give the firm the competitive advantage of a targeted activity, or the reduced risk of a generic one. An example would be the Social Media Site reducing emissions, or the Bakery planting trees. From purely a social perspective, it's important not to discourage these activities, and I would certainly not want to imply that firms should only bother addressing one or two social problems.

From a pragmatic CSR perspective on the other hand, I would phrase it slightly differently. Yes, companies should try to be as socially beneficial as they can be, but they should prioritise using their resources to tackle the key issues of their industry. If they're then still able to engage in other activities, then that's obviously beneficial, but only if doing so doesn't reduce their ability to contribute to their more specific social mission. Like all facets of CSR, balance plays a key part.

Overall, I'd say that it's only by realising the effects and consequences of their activities that a company will be in a prime position to increase or readjust resource allocation accordingly. Equally, I think it's only by using this type of method that companies will begin to comprehend CSR as a truly strategic discipline, making it pragmatic enough to finally be taken seriously.

4

Runaway Train

Imagine a world where one of the first things that entered your mind when you thought of a particular brand or company was whether or not they positively influenced society. In such a utopia, deciding what to buy and where to buy it would be quite a pleasant experience, and you'd feel really good about yourself afterwards. I can't help but think that we'd all be a bit more peaceful and a little less wrapped up in materialism and consumerism irrespective of the consequences. While at the moment, we may be nowhere near such a situation, it seems reasonable to point out that we can only get there by strengthening the underlying trust relationship between companies and consumers. Having already spoken about targeted CSR, the remaining two criteria for success that must be met are integration and communication. In essence, both of these ideas are heavily connected, as they both help to develop the type of corporate reputation that turns hypothetical purchasing intention into tangible revenue. However, as I've briefly touched upon, it could be argued that the two concepts are simply different stages of a broader method for improving said reputation.

To understand this, let's ask ourselves the following question: Why is it that our default response to companies such as Ben and Jerry's and The Body Shop differs from a company like McDonald's? McDonald's currently have a pretty comprehensive TV campaign dispelling all the myths about their farming practices, but I can't help continue to see Ben and Jerry's and The Body Shop as more responsible companies, even with perhaps less knowledge of their actual activities. If consumers are looking for ethical/responsible places to eat, they may stay away from Nando's (after their tax avoidance was made public), but will McDonald's spring to mind as quickly as The Body Shop does when looking for a responsible cosmetics company? I think this observation demonstrates the earlier idea that CSR can't be truly 'successful' without meeting all three of previously stated criteria. With this in mind, what can companies do to transition towards creating a reputation that is as positive as The Body Shop's? To try and make sure that this book remains practically useful, I will do my very best to answer this question. Firstly, however, I think it's worthwhile going on a bit of a wild tangent to truly understand why such a transition is so beneficial.

To do this, we have to delve a little bit into the mind-bending world of ethics and philosophy. It might seem slightly less relevant at the moment, but with any luck, it will all come together in the end. The more I think about it, the more surprised I am that it's taken me until chapter four to bring the idea of ethics into the CSR discussion. After all, Business Ethics is another phrase often used interchangeably with CSR, and the whole notion of morality forms the basis of most arguments in favour of it. Perhaps in that sense, this chapter will differ slightly from the others. While so far I have talked about CSR as necessary for organisations to succeed, primarily due to consumers caring about it, I'll now suggest that CSR is also simply the 'right' thing to do. I've deliberately approached the concept of right and wrong with caution. Largely because, on a practical level at least, it's of little use to businesses. If consumers are starting to demand that businesses are socially responsible, then businesses will need to take that feedback on board if they want to succeed. So far, that's been enough of a reason to argue that businesses should bother with it, and I like to think the ideas I've introduced provide a practical way for businesses to do just that. However, even by taking the proactive approach I spoke about in the last chapter, companies may still run the risk of being just another organisation that does 'responsible things', instead of being a truly 'responsible organisation'.

So, to somehow try and tackle this notion of what is 'right' and what is 'wrong', we need to start at the very beginning, addressing a core philosophical debate regarding consequentialism. As the name suggests, the consequentialism discussion rests solely on the value that we choose to assign to the consequences of our, or other people's, actions. These ideas are quite commonly presented by asking whether or not 'the ends justify the means'. As we know, the 'ends' in this phrase refer to the consequences, and the 'means' are whatever actions are taken to bring about those consequences. In theory, the topic of consequentialism is quite polarising; either you think that doing something bad to achieve something good is worth it, or you think you should just try and be good and whatever will be, will be. Perhaps this is an oversimplification, but I'm no philosopher, and I'm not particularly interested in answering these questions objectively. After all, everybody has their individual moral compass, and I'm in no position to try and recalibrate them all. For all I know, maybe my moral compass is the one that needs recalibrating. Anyway, while I don't intend to 'solve' these conundrums, I do intend to apply them to the corporate world to see if there is a logical rationale for companies to approach CSR in a certain way, but more about that later.

If you're currently reading this wondering whether you think you're a consequentialist (somebody that cares about the result rather than how you got there) or a non-consequentialist (somebody who doesn't worry about results, but how you achieve them), here's a little thought experiment for you. It's a very well known example, and I believe it's used in interviews at some top universities to understand the way students approach complex issues. It's known colloquially as 'the trolley problem' and goes something like this:

A runaway train is heading down the tracks and is set to hit five workers who are doing maintenance work. For whatever reason, you can't warn them that the train is coming and they are completely unaware of the danger they are in. In short, they face certain death in just a few moments. However, there is one thing you can do. Instead of just watching this horror unfold, you are fortunately positioned right next to a crucial lever. By pulling the lever, you can divert the train onto a different track, saving the five workers. The only catch (wasn't it all sounding a bit too easy?), is that on the second track there is one worker, in a similar situation of helplessness. By pulling the lever, the train will kill the one man but save the five. Would you pull it?

Most people in this situation would say yes, which may or may not come as a surprise to you. Now let's imagine there is no lever, but an entirely different opportunity available to you. You could still stop the train hitting the five workers, but this time you must push an extremely large man off a bridge, with his sheer size stopping the train. What would you do in this situation?

A true consequentialist, or a 'utilitarian', would argue that both the 'lever pulling' and the 'fat man pushing' are indistinguishable acts. Both actions will kill one man and save five. Consequentially, that is undeniably the best outcome (unless you want to start getting all abstract and suggest that certain lives are worth more than others). If you're interested, most people tend to say that they would pull the lever but not push the man. Some people might even argue that pulling the lever is just as bad as pushing the man, meaning both actions are equally inadvisable, and you should let the train kill the five in both circumstances.

Given that the five workers seem completely unaware of their impending doom, and are unknowingly relying on spectators to save their lives, I'd be tempted to agree, but that's beside the point.

In short, what this thought experiment really highlights is that nobody sits on either one of the two extremes. If the consequences are super important to us, we'll probably be willing to do more 'bad' things in order to achieve them than if the consequences didn't matter as much. It's all a matter of context. As we drift through life, we make all these moral decisions on a case by case basis, and slowly but surely that starts to create what we would describe as our personal sense of morality, our very own idea of what is 'right' and what is 'wrong'. The good thing about this is that it saves people the time of trying to argue solely in favour of one of the two ideals. Such a debate might be an interesting academic exercise, but it would mean very little when applied to real life. With this in mind, when I start to apply the notion of 'right' and 'wrong' to CSR and corporate behaviour, what I'm essentially going to do is discuss two possible situations.

Firstly, are there some instances where the consequences are so overwhelmingly positive that any negative means by which companies achieve them no longer matter? Similarly, are there instances where the means that are so overwhelmingly negative that any positive consequences no longer matter? If we can start to make some headway in addressing these two questions, we can begin to give CSR the moral component that it undoubtedly deserves.

Perhaps it's a mistake to suggest that we can answer these two questions individually. In reality, it's entirely possible to look at specific situations and answer both at the same time. The case I have in mind relates predominantly to large multinational organisations. A company like Unilever might be a good example. Unilever, for those that don't know, is one of the most powerful fast moving consumer goods (FCMG) companies in the world. They are the parent company behind brands like Dove, Vaseline, Hellman's and countless others. On a side note, if you've never looked into the parent companies that own and manage the brands we buy, it's worth a bit of your time. It's very easy for us to forget that a small minority of companies have such a large amount of power, owning the majority of everything we purchase on a regular basis. Oxfam made an excellent infographic about this exact idea, consequently claiming that only ten companies in the world own pretty much everything that we might see in a supermarket. Between them, they make over $1bn a day in revenue. It's well worth a Google.

Anyway, that's not why I wanted to talk about Unilever. From a CSR perspective, huge companies like Unilever represent a complicated issue. Having started operating in the late 19th century, Unilever steadily grew before rapidly becoming a household name shortly after the 1950s and 60s. As I spoke about way back in chapter one, CSR was barely even a concept in those days, and the idea of businesses having social obligations was still a couple of decades away from being widely adopted. It seems reasonable then to assume that Unilever's growth came more from focusing on lowering costs and maximising profit, than by actively engaging in CSR activities. That's not to suggest with any certainty that Unilever were socially irresponsible during this time, but it seems pretty likely that they benefitted from a general lack of consensus that businesses should also help society.

In short, there are bound to be some examples of times where Unilever operated in ways which we would view as undesirable in today's world. A prime example might have been usage of raw material and natural resources. When scarcity was less of an urgent issue, Unilever probably didn't spend much time worrying too much about what things might be like in 60 or 70 years' time. Fast forward to 2018 however, and Unilever are unquestionably one of the more responsible companies around, especially within the FCMG industry. In 2010, Unilever launched the Unilever Sustainable Living Plan (USLP), and it now influences the vast majority of their operations on a global level.

So where am I going with this? Well, how often have you heard of companies deciding that they're going to 'give something back' to society? For me, it seems like an all too familiar pledge. It's also a pledge I find quite bizarre. As I briefly mentioned earlier, I often find myself wondering if rather than giving something back, they would have been better off simply not taking it in the first place. On a wider corporate level, this sort of behaviour seems quite common. Larger, and usually older, companies, which in some way or another have benefitted from ungoverned growth in a completely different commercial context, are suddenly coming out of the woodwork offering to 'give something back'. The question I then find myself asking is, is that enough? Is it okay for companies to grow as a result of irresponsible behaviour, only to then start being responsible as and when they can spare the resources? To explain this further, I think it's necessary to work through a more complete, and sadly numerical, scenario.

Say you have a company that has just started out. As a result of starting up at a time when CSR barely existed, they can get away with some questionable business practices. These business practices, (e.g. unfair wages, poor working conditions etc.) help them to outcompete their rivals and start to grow. Let's just say that the way they are operating results in a net negative effect on society of -10. Obviously, assigning a value is completely impossible, but it will help to understand the concept a bit more clearly. Now imagine, after ten years of irresponsibility, the company is now big enough to spare some resources for CSR. By this point, those ten years have amounted to a net negative societal influence of -100. However, now the company is a household name, it can afford to be more responsible. Maybe now, their annual net effect on society is positive, let's say +20. After five years of being responsible, their net impact on society will be zero, and after ten years their net effect on society will become +100. Again, it's worth mentioning that the numbers are not significant in this example. All that's important is the idea that companies, in theory, could have grown in a way that is irresponsible, to then start being responsible once they have the resources available, effectively 'making up' for their behaviour in the past. The question we can then ask, is at what point is this acceptable?

A far more dramatic and historical example could be slavery in America in the 19th century. As a result of slavery, U.S. cotton was extremely competitive, accounting for over half of America's exports. The U.S. grew over 60% of the world's cotton, and slave labour unarguably contributed to the economic development they have enjoyed in the years and decades since. Going back to the two questions relating to consequences, are we prepared to say that America's economic growth is a consequence so beneficial, that slavery was worth it? Or are we going to take the view that slavery was so morally wrong that no amount of economic growth could justify it? As much as I'd like to think most of us would adopt the latter viewpoint, I'm almost certain that the former opinion is equally existent.

The growth of modern corporations, therefore, while hopefully less morally extreme, requires a similar amount of scrutiny. If a clothing company has become successful by using child labour to undercut competitors, what level of CSR is then needed for consumers to be willing to see their past behaviour as worthwhile? These kind of questions are unbelievably difficult to ask, let alone answer, but they're worth thinking about nonetheless. Unfortunately, the situation becomes even more complicated when we bring another company into the hypothetical example we used earlier.

Let's say this new company wants to be as socially responsible as possible from day one. They want their whole business to revolve around it. Because this company has just started out, they won't have many resources to dedicate to being socially responsible, so maybe their annual net effect on society is something like +2. Again, the numbers are merely there to demonstrate the point that the smaller company's capacity for CSR will be lower than the previous company that only started CSR once they were already a household name. After five years, this company has only had a net social impact of +10.

What may have happened if this company started up in a time when CSR was less valued, is that they wouldn't have survived past their 5th year. By trying to be as socially responsible as possible, they might not have been price competitive, and consumers wouldn't have valued CSR enough to make it sustainable. This is where it gets difficult. Is it more socially beneficial for a company to grow irresponsibly, to then be responsible on a large scale, or for a company to try and be responsible from day one, but never grow or even survive at all?

Before CSR was taken seriously and demanded on some level by consumers, this was precisely the kind of moral sacrifice that existed. However, as I mentioned earlier, there's no point in me trying to put forward a definitive answer, because no such solution can ever exist. Morality, by definition, is subjective and means something slightly different to everyone. What I think I can do, however, is discuss the possible next steps that different types of businesses can take.

Okay, so it's certainly possible that some of the most prominent companies that exist today got to the position they are in without having to worry too much about society. In reality, there's very little anybody, including the companies themselves, can do about that. They can't go back in time and change things, and even if they could, another company would no doubt be in their place instead. The growth of many of these companies stems back to the fact that the corporate system in place at the time incentivised profit maximisation, irrespective of social cost. All these companies can realistically do, and all that consumers can therefore reasonably demand is that from now on, they at least use their vast array of resources as positively as they can. It's at this point that we should revisit the phrase 'giving something back'. If, for example, I stole £10,000 from a friend, leaving them financially ruined for several months, only to go on to turn that £10,000 into £10,000,000, I'd probably need to give that friend a fair bit more than the original £10,000 I stole if I wanted to win them over again. Similarly, it makes sense that companies need to go a bit further than simply making amends for some of the things they might have got away with in the past.

This is where the idea of integration comes in. It's this 'giving something back' logic that makes CSR quite granular. It makes it less about sincerity and more about a series of token gestures to win over the public. What therefore needs to happen, is for companies to fully integrate the issues that can be identified from the previous chapter into the DNA of their organisation. What I mean by this, is that companies need to effectively place similar value in societal targets as they do in financial ones. They need to make sure that their business exists to help society in ways that aren't just economic, and they need every part of their business to share the underlying vision.

Unilever is a great example of this. The scope of the USLP is incredibly broad, involving all global subsidiaries and the divisions within them. It still focusses on addressing specific social issues, but they've made those issues influence their behaviour in every business area. Whether it's Marketing or Supply Chain, the USLP is so deeply integrated into their corporate identity, that you'll struggle to find an employee that isn't, in some way or another, on board with it. This is the process that M&S is currently going through with their Plan A initiative. The crux of the idea is fantastic, but I think that they have a little bit further to go before it's as integrated as the USLP is within Unilever. However, it is these types of enduring CSR ambitions that companies need to create if they want to be truly known as a socially responsible organisation.

So, if deeper integration of CSR is so crucial, how do companies go about achieving it? Well, you could probably argue that there are multiple methods for integrating CSR, but undoubtedly the most effective is through senior management participation and promotion. At the end of the day, if the CEO and other company directors are committed to tackling social issues, then it will very quickly start to filter down into all areas of the business. Again, M&S and Unilever are prime examples of this working in practice. After eight successful quarters of decline in the fashion sector, M&S boss Marc Bolland said that their Plan A programme was 'integral' to the company's rebirth. For a CEO to tell investors that a CSR initiative is the most important factor for reversing their poor fortunes, it's no surprise that it quickly started to be taken very seriously. Likewise, Unilever CEO Paul Polman has been interviewed numerous times about social issues. Each time, he passionately speaks about having the 'moral courage' to address social issues. When the most powerful individual in a global company sees CSR as invaluable, it reverberates around the rest of the corporate hierarchy. While getting senior managers on board can sometimes be hard work, you need only look at these types of business leaders to realise just how fruitful such an approach can be.

Overall, the point I'm making is that no matter how hard we try, the general public can't do anything about how organisations may or may not have behaved in the past. All they can do is hope and demand that they act better in the future. Instead of just being happy with a few token gestures, consumers should, and no doubt will, start to demand a bit more. As CSR becomes more and more important, individual acts of responsibility won't be half as valuable as genuinely responsible companies, and consumers will start to be able to tell the difference.

For larger companies then, integration should hopefully seem necessary, but what about the small and medium-sized enterprises (SMEs)? After all, SMEs account for over 99% of all businesses, so where do they fit into all this?

Well, remember the hypothetical example of the company who struggled to survive by trying to be as socially responsible as possible from day one? Fortunately, such an outcome is becoming less and less likely. Companies that embed some form of social or environmental ambition from the get-go are rapidly increasing in popularity. A great example is a company I mentioned in a previous chapter, a mattress start-up called Leesa. While I didn't think that their action of planting a tree for every sale was particularly well targeted, they also vow to donate a mattress to a homeless shelter for every ten they sell, and they have done ever since they started up. These new 'social enterprises' are popping up all over the place, and their newfound success rates are as good a reason as any for why integrating CSR into a newer/smaller business could form a great platform from which they can build. A recent study found that 66% of social enterprises survived their first five years of operation, compared to 47% of traditional businesses. With CSR rapidly gaining traction with consumers, companies looking to grow should seriously consider connecting their business to a social or environmental mission.

What I've effectively tried to demonstrate throughout this chapter, is that irrespective of size, companies have both a moral obligation and an upcoming commercial incentive to adopt, and integrate, CSR. To briefly go back to consumers, it's the companies with deeply embedded social values that will be viewed in the most positive light.

However, so far throughout this book, I've maintained the view that consumers are starting to care more and more about CSR. Given the number of studies that support this idea, it's hardly incorrect, but it does imply that consumers make purchasing decisions in a very logical, rational way. You only need to read a bit about purchasing psychology to learn that very rarely do we adopt such a systematic process. It is here that we can make the final justification for integrated CSR. In reality, while some consumers will consciously seek out responsible companies to purchase from, most of us will tend not to think about it as comprehensively. When we want to buy something, individual companies and brands will pop into our mind, and the decision is probably made before we're even conscious of it.

If CSR exists only as a selection of 'gestures' and isolated activities, then it might be enough to sway the extremely rational decision makers, but it won't be enough to win over those of us they make decisions more automatically. This is why integration is so essential. It's only through an integrated CSR strategy that a positive corporate reputation for social responsibility can be developed. That's why companies like The Body Shop and Ben & Jerry's (owned by Unilever) have such strong reputations. It is those types of reputations that will put companies straight into the mind of the subconscious, yet socially driven, consumer, allowing organisations to use CSR as a genuine tool for both social change and business success.

5

The Famous Chick

I like to think of myself as a 'good' person. I've given to various charities over the years, I sign the odd petition for worthwhile causes, and I give blood every three months. On top of that, I haven't committed any serious crimes, and while being a 'good' person shouldn't just be a case of not killing anyone, surely that counts for something. Don't get me wrong, my daily routine doesn't revolve around anxiously waiting for news of my knighthood to come through the post (if that's even how it works), but I'd say on the whole, I do more good than harm. On top of that, I occasionally like to tell people about some of the things I do. Giving blood is a prime example. Giving blood is something I deeply care about, and even though the donation centres are always pretty busy, there is always more demand for blood than there is supply. What I sometimes do then, is talk about giving blood, so that maybe the people I'm speaking to will think that they should do it too. I think we can all agree that doing so is quite a beneficial exercise. However, I can't deny that a little bit of me feels quite good about telling people. I get a certain amount of enjoyment out of other people thinking I'm a 'good' person, which I've convinced myself is only natural. However, if I let this little part of me take over, and I start dedicating my life to telling everybody how amazing I am for giving blood, it is probably more likely to annoy them than encourage them to do the same. This phenomenon is why communicating CSR is a bit of a minefield. Get it right, and you can have some genuine positive influence, get it wrong, and you can alienate the very people you are trying to impress.

Perhaps this is the reason why companies so often neglect effective communication of CSR activities. To be fair, it's not necessarily the case that organisations overlook it entirely, more that they approach it which such caution that the majority of attempts are mostly ineffective. On the face of it, I don't think we can blame companies for such an approach. Granted, they may benefit from a glowing corporate reputation if they told us about how great they are, but if consumers think it's all a PR stunt, it will have the complete opposite effect. What's more, companies that come across as insincere with their CSR might have a tough job trying to win the public back over by convincing everybody how much they actually do care about the issues they're tackling. As with all forms of reputation, it's far easier for a positive reputation to quickly turn negative than for a negative reputation to quickly turn positive.

By looking a bit deeper into CSR communication, you'll find that the root of the problem is far more inherent and, to some extent, unavoidable. After all, if a company wants to communicate their CSR activity, they essentially have two fundamental goals that they seek to accomplish. Firstly, they want whoever sees or reads their content to think of the company in a more positive light. Naturally, all forms of corporate communication exist for that primary purpose. However, as well as that, the company will also be hoping that you feel so overwhelmingly connected to whatever it is they have put out, that you'll want to tell as many different people about it as you possibly can. Realistically speaking, both of these aims are merely different stages of achieving the overarching goal of increasing sales. What's the point of everybody thinking how great a particular company is if nobody is willing to buy from them? Increased sales are, therefore, the ultimate focus.

Where this becomes problematic is that when communicating CSR, companies need to somehow make consumers think that they're not just saying how responsible they are so that they increase sales. From a consumer perspective, there are few things worse than companies trying to convince you that they're helping society, just so you can part with your money, only to later realise that they're nowhere near as responsible as they made out. Therefore, if a company manages to show that they're not just doing CSR for sales, then, providing they're successful, they'll probably end up getting some. However, if a company is deliberately trying to not focus on sales, just so customers think they are sincere and then buy from them, then aren't they still doing it for the wrong reasons?

I wouldn't be at all surprised if you're confused. The whole situation is a complete paradox. Realistically, you could argue that if companies genuinely cared about social issues, they wouldn't feel the need to publicise what they're doing to tackle them at all. The problem is, if companies don't broadcast what they're doing, they won't be able to financially benefit from their CSR, which means they might be unable to sustain it, and we'll be back to a situation where the most irresponsible companies make the most money. All in all, the world of CSR communication exists on a knife-edge between success and failure. It's no wonder that companies try and tackle it at arm's length. However, while this challenge has always existed to some extent, it's impossible to discuss it any further without addressing perhaps the most important factor that is making it even harder for firms to overcome: social media.

There is no disputing the truly seismic way that social media has shaped the way we live our lives. You could argue for an eternity on whether this change has been for better or for worse, but you can't deny that the change has occurred. In what perhaps sounds like a scary proposition, the truth of the matter is that social media, in many ways, holds all the cards. Without it, consumers would probably not value CSR anywhere near as much as they do. After all, CSR has primarily gained traction due to the average consumer becoming more educated and informed about what goes on behind closed doors to get their favourite products into their hands. Issues like child labour in clothing factories could have stayed a corporate secret if social media never came along. Of course, you could argue that better communication technology in general has facilitated this newfound transparency between company and consumer, but social media has given it the necessary traction. Through platforms like Facebook, Twitter and YouTube, every person with an internet connection is effectively mobilised as an investigative journalist, and it's far harder for organisations to hide from that many prying eyes.

Perhaps more notably though, is the possibility to go 'viral'. The unbelievable speed in which stories can spread around the world should be a cause for both unprecedented excitement and unprecedented fear when it comes to the world of business. Get on the right side of the wave, and the benefits are massive, but get on the wrong side, and the whole world is talking about it before the company has even made a statement. It's this phenomenon that has massively amplified the consequences, both positive and negative, of a company's marketing strategy.

Throughout this chapter then, I aim to provide some meaningful guidance, along with real-life examples, to help demonstrate how companies can communicate CSR in a way that makes the minefield a little bit easier to traverse. Don't get me wrong, it's never going to be a walk in the park, but there are definitely some things that companies can do to maximise their chances of success. Going right back to basics, the first hurdle for companies to overcome when marketing CSR is understanding the value that consumers place on it. Before a firm can even try and engage with people, they need a solid understanding of what they care about, how much they care about it, and how they want you to communicate it.

I like to think I've already answered the first one of those challenges. When we looked at targeted CSR back in chapter three, we were able to see that generally speaking, people assigned significant importance on whether or not particular social issues were relevant to the company's industry. If therefore, a company like Toyota started telling the world about how they're helping the homeless, they'll probably be less successful than if they told the world about how they're reducing harmful emissions. Remember, that's not to say that helping the homeless is in anyway bad, it just won't necessarily resonate with automotive customers as much as tackling emissions will. So, with that in mind, we can move onto the harder issue of trying to find out just how much customers care about these issues.

This is a hugely beneficial exercise when it comes to marketing, as it can help companies understand what the balance might be between CSR and non-CSR related content. After all, if a company's customers don't value CSR at all, then it wouldn't make sense for 30% of their marketing material to be CSR related. On the other hand, if CSR is hugely important, only dedicating 1% of resources to CSR content won't impress them too much. Unfortunately, no magical figure will work every time, but by looking at some research I've conducted, companies might be able to get a rough idea.

Just before I share the results of this particular study, I should probably explain what caused me to create it in the first place. As I mentioned previously, the vast majority of CSR research surrounds whether people care about it in general, and how that varies between specific demographics or has changed over time. For a long time, I've felt that such information isn't as useful as perhaps it could be. I found myself wondering if there was a way we could start to put a value on just how much consumers really care, so I set out to try and do just that.

The study, in essence, was incredibly straightforward. To try and quantify how much value people placed on social responsibility, I wanted to understand the premium that they were willing to pay for it. When other bits of research ended with the simple conclusion that people are prepared to pay more, I wanted to see how much more, and how that 'multiplier' changed with different groups of people. To try and do this I created a really simple survey. Respondents were asked four questions, all practically identical. The only difference was that each question gave them a price for a different type of product. They then had to answer how much they would pay for that exact product if it came from a socially responsible company or was made in a socially responsible way. It was important to stress that the level of CSR associated with the product was the only thing that could alter how much they would be willing to pay for it. The design and quality of the product would be the same in both instances.

These were the products and prices that I gave to them, based on rough average market prices at the time:

Product	Price
Tin of Instant Coffee	£2
Pair of Jeans	£30
Smartphone	£300
Car	£15,000

It was crucial that the four products in the study were of varying prices, as it would help me test my first hypothesis. Due to the price inelasticity of cheaper items, I would expect the CSR multiplier, or premium, to be far higher for the coffee than the car. After all, paying 50% extra for coffee only amounts to £1, but paying 50% extra for the car is £7,500. While this seemed pretty obvious, I wanted to test it nonetheless. On top of that, I wanted to get a sense for how the CSR multipliers varied dependant on gender, age and income. The reason I chose these three factors is that they're arguably the main ones that companies use to identify their target market. If I could see how perceptions of CSR changed based on these factors, then companies could apply the conclusions when marketing their products to specific groups of people.

Overall, the study recorded results from over 800 consumers, and fortunately, the conclusions suggest that my time and effort was somewhat worthwhile. Firstly, when collating all the entries, I was able to prove the first hypothesis very quickly. Also, I was able to deduce the usual bits of data that CSR research tends to provide. For example, from the entire set of respondents, 58.25% of them said that they would pay more for at least one of the four products.

To get a sense of how much those people valued it, I analysed the data from *just* those that said they would pay more and took an average of the premiums. The table below shows the average percentage increase that consumers who care about CSR would be willing to pay for each of the products if they had a CSR component.

Product	Price	Premium for CSR
Tin of Instant Coffee	£2	46.38%
Pair of Jeans	£30	28.17%
Smartphone	£300	16.54%
Car	£15,000	10.20%

As you can quite clearly see, the cheaper the product, the higher the CSR premium. Other than the clear financial reason for this, I think it also makes sense when looking at it from another angle. Generally speaking, as products increase in value, the level of differentiation increases. Cheaper products such as instant coffee can't really be differentiated as easily, so consumers are more willing to use something like CSR to do it for them. Cars, on the other hand, vary hugely from brand to brand, so CSR is less likely to be as valuable for consumers making decisions. Sure, they might be happy paying a little bit more for it, but factors like design and other features will be the primary selling points. From a communication and marketing standpoint, I think this data shows that companies selling cheap, fast moving products, have a fantastic opportunity to incorporate CSR content into their communication strategy, but more on that later.

At this point, we have established the base multiplier levels, so it is now necessary to look at how they varied by demographic. As implied earlier on, I'm going to split this into three different sections, focusing first on Age, Gender, and finally, Income.

Age

One of the most significant conclusions to have come out of CSR research is that young people value it enormously. This was something I was keen to explore for myself, and my study provided the ideal means from which to do so. Before looking at the results, it's necessary to say that from this point onward, there are two key bits of data to pay attention to. Firstly, the % of people in each age group that value CSR at all, and secondly, how the amount they value it by changes as people get older. The data in the table below helps answer the first of those questions. Remember, the following percentages relate to the number of people within each age group that said they would be prepared to pay a higher price for at least one of the four products.

Age Group	*% of People Willing to Pay a Premium*
18-30	74%
31-45	51%
46-65	54%

As predicted, the data in the above table highlights what many others have concluded by demonstrating that a significantly higher proportion of people in the 18-30 age group are prepared to pay more for socially responsible products than their older counterparts. This further concreates the commonly made claim that the current and future generations are the most socially conscious ever.

To answer the second question however, I needed to see how the premiums differed for each product according to these age groups. Once again, to get this data I took *only* the answers from those who said they would pay more for each product, as that was the only way to find out just how much the people who do care about CSR, value it. The table below shows the results:

Age	CSR Premium			
	Car	Phone	Jeans	Coffee
18-30	11.35%	18.46%	31.51%	62.68%
31-45	11.50%	18.10%	26.69%	44.00%
46-65	8.46%	14.57%	27.50%	52.95%

I appreciate that the table above is a bit of an explosion of percentages, but I think some fascinating insights can be drawn from it. For starters, the CSR premiums for the 18-30 group are above the average ones (from a couple of pages ago) in all four products. The 31-45 group is only above average in two of the four products, and the 46-65 group is only above for one product (unsurprisingly the Coffee). The second observation surrounds what happens to the perceived value of CSR as the consumer's age increases. Have a look at the premiums for the 18-30 group and the 31-45 group. Do you notice how, with the exception of the coffee, they're pretty similar? This fact can help us deduce a very useful conclusion.

When it comes to moving from the 18-30 age group into the 31-45 age group, the problem isn't that people value CSR less, it's that fewer people value it all all. After all, only 51% of 31-45 year-olds would pay more for CSR, compared to 74% of 18-30 year-olds. Of those that would, however, the premiums are mostly equal. The complete opposite is the case when we move from from the 31-45 group to the 46-65 bracket. This time, a similar number people care about CSR in general, but of those who do, they value it less (particularly among more expensive products). It's this type of understanding that could be useful for companies that target most of their products to a single age group.

Income

Generally speaking, people tend to earn more money as they get older. For all I knew, the table of premiums related to age was merely due to wealthier people not valuing CSR, as opposed to it being related in any way to people getting older. To try and address this issue, I created an identical table, this time looking at how personal income affected the values. To try and get statistically significant data, I only looked at income groups where I had a sufficient sample size. In essence, the under 10k bracket represents low earners, the 20-30k bracket represents median earners, and the 40k+ bracket represents high earners. The results were as follows:

Personal Income	*% of People Willing to Pay a Premium*
Under 10k	54%
20-30k	60%
40k+	60%

And of those willing to pay more, the premiums were as follows:

Personal Income	CSR Premium			
	Car	Phone	Jeans	Coffee
Under 10k	9.20%	15.47%	26.82%	44.81%
20-30k	11.70%	20.59%	29.04%	44.82%
40k+	8.75%	14.72%	25.75%	35.36%

Given the sample size, we can say that the % of people willing to pay more for CSR is mostly similar across income groups. Yes, the low income group had a slightly lower percentage, but that's probably due to lacking the financial means to pay anything other than the base price. What's more interesting, therefore, is the pattern that we can see in the second table. In essence, the value of CSR goes up as you go from low earners to median earners but then goes down from median earners to high earners. Potentially this is related to age, but it's equally possible that a median income exists in the 'sweet spot' between being young enough to be more socially conscious while being wealthy enough to translate that desire into specific purchasing intentions.

Gender

Finally, the last criterion to look at is gender. Given the widespread stereotype that women are more caring and selfless, whereas men are perhaps more ruthless and self-centred, I was interested to see if such a stereotype would ring true with regards to CSR. Using the same two tables as before, we can see the results quite clearly:

Gender	% of People Willing to Pay a Premium
Male	54%
Female	61%

Whilst the difference is slight, it could certainly be argued that women are slightly more responsive to CSR than men. However, as we saw with different age brackets, that doesn't always affect the actual premiums. To see if this was also the case with gender, the following table looks the the individual multipliers for each of the four products:

Gender	CSR Premium			
	Car	Phone	Jeans	Coffee
Male	8.97%	13.86%	25.80%	39.57%
Female	10.94%	15.81%	30.52%	43.38%

As you can see, for every product, women said they would pay more for the responsible product on average than men would. Admittedly the differences aren't monumental, but they're significant enough to suggest a slight gender bias when it comes to planning a CSR marketing strategy.

Speaking of which, how does all of this information help companies in any way when it comes to communicating CSR? For this, it's important not to get hung up on the exact prices that people have said they are willing to pay. As I spoke about in an earlier chapter, these kinds of studies only record purchasing intention, which is very different from actual purchasing behaviour. What it does do, however, is give some insight into roughly how much people value CSR in general. If Kenco knew that people appreciate CSR enough to spend nearly 50% more on their products, they would probably market it even more than they currently do. Even more importantly though, is looking at the general conclusions we can draw about which groups of people value CSR the most. From the study, we can suggest that women value it slightly more than men, that young people value it more than older people, and that middle earners value it more than low and high earners. Depending on a company's target market, this kind of information could help encourage a firm to take the plunge with some cause-related marketing and see whether or not it pays off.

An example of this working in real life is a social media post made by Dawn, maker of a popular washing up liquid, in 2016. Dawn wanted to communicate that their washing up liquid was great for removing grease, but didn't harm any animals when it entered the water system. They posted a photo on Facebook that contained a pair of hands doing the washing up, gently holding a baby chick. Try and find it if you can, it's extremely cute.

If we were to analyse this form of CSR, we would realise that it ticks pretty much all of the boxes. Firstly, the issue they are tackling is directly related to the industry. Secondly, while Dawn is just a brand owned by Procter and Gamble, the social ambition of saving wildlife is something that they've deeply integrated. It's plastered all over their website, and they've been working on the issue for over 30 years, partnering with The Marine Mammal Centre and International Bird Rescue in the process. Finally, from that data I've just discussed, we know that consumers are far more receptive to CSR when it comes to cheap, everyday products. On paper then, it looks like their baby chick CSR related post should have been successful. So what happened?

Well, in short, 708,000 likes happened, 47,000 shares happened, and 15,000 comments happened. It was one of the most successful CSR driven Facebook posts ever put out by a company. When you consider that fact that Dawn only have just over 1 million page likes, getting so many on just one post is practically unheard of.

What I hope the information presented throughout this chapter can help to do is highlight that, like Dawn, it is entirely possible for companies to get CSR marketing absolutely spot on.

However, I must admit that there are two more factors that influenced Dawn's success that I haven't yet touched on, these are: choosing the right type of communication platform, and anchoring their claim to honesty.

To address the first point, and going back to what I've already said about social media, it's vital that companies present CSR in the way that consumers want to learn about it. In the 80s and 90s, all that companies could do was publish some form of CSR report, which I would imagine only a very dedicated handful of consumers would ever read. If you ask me, the entire concept of a CSR report, for anybody other than shareholders, press and future business partners, is becoming redundant. Consumers will almost never read it, and it will probably take far more effort to put together than a simple Facebook post. When we look back at the data surrounding young people, it's clear that engaging with them is crucial to long-term business success. Social media is almost the exclusive way to do this. Not only does it provide a method of giving young people the rapidly updating information that they're after, but it also provides an excellent platform for turning traditional 'one-way' marketing into a new 'two-way' discussion.

If companies respond and react to the views of consumers, they'll be in a much better position when it comes to getting people to take them seriously. If companies don't harness social media, they'll never acquire the responsible reputation that they're looking for, and you can be pretty sure that a competitor will beat them to it. This book is not going to delve too deep into how to use social media as effectively as possible; there are plenty of other books that focus entirely on that. All I'll say is that it has to be the primary platform for communicating CSR, as that is the home of the consumers that businesses are so eager to impress.

The second point is just as important, and it relates to ensuring that any CSR marketing activity is directly related to truth. Remember right at the start of this chapter when I spoke about being on the right side of the line between sincerity and a PR stunt? Telling the truth is a definite step in the right direction when it comes to doing so. There are numerous examples of companies that have underestimated this, thinking they can get away with a slight over exaggeration or manipulation of data. If there's one thing to learn it's that socially conscious consumers can't be easily fooled. They'll always be somebody looking to trip a company up, and if they do, there's every chance it could be halfway around the world before they can even press delete.

Despite this, plenty of companies still give it a go, often to make up for their lack of actual CSR activity. A 2015 article coined a particularly good phrase for this sort of practice, called 'Virtue Signalling'. This phrase pretty much relates to any instance where a company, or an individual for that matter, says or does certain things to make them sound far more virtuous than they actually are. I think it's quite telling that this phrase has caught on like wildfire, as the vast majority of people have probably been guilty of it at one time or another. In short, companies must avoid such a label like the plague, as their reputation with the future generation could very much depend on it.

It may seem like companies have to tick a lot of boxes to get CSR communication right, but I don't think any of them are particularly unreasonable. If companies have already met the criteria of targeting and integrating, then all they have to do is understand what their customers care about, harness the power of social media, and make sure they tell the truth. Is that really too much to ask?

6

Ticking Boxes

What do Strawberries and Cream, Macaroni and Cheese and Salt and Pepper all have in common? They're all much better together than they are apart. I like to think in some way or another I've made a similar point with all of the CSR principles that I've introduced. Going way back to chapter two, the three foundations of targeting, integrating and communicating must all come together for a company's CSR strategy to be as successful as possible. Hopefully, in the three chapters that followed, the importance of these principles was made clear, but do they hold up to scrutiny when applied to some real-world examples? That is what this chapter is about.

It's one thing to logically agree with the frameworks I have proposed; it's another thing entirely to see them working in action. It's only then that companies and entrepreneurs will truly start to adopt them. In the last chapter, I used them to break down the main reasons why Dawn's social media CSR post was so successful. It ticked all the boxes I've been going on about, and they deserved to reap the rewards. However, with CSR, and life in general I suppose, it's far easier to learn from other's mistakes than their successes. For whatever reason, we prefer to look at examples of failure and think 'I'll be fine as long as I don't do that' than look at examples of success and think 'I'll be fine if I just do what they've done'. Learning from failure is far more actionable. Fortunately, for us at least, there are countless examples of monumental corporate cock-ups that could single-handedly write the world's biggest CSR textbook. By taking a look at some of them in more detail and pinpointing exactly where it all went wrong, you'll be able to see precisely how each failure could have been avoided.

Perhaps the word 'failure' isn't always the right word in these cases. Sure, there are some corporate disasters for which the word 'failure' is being generous, but it's not just those examples that I want to look at. When a company gets something so fundamentally wrong, it's pretty easy to pick out a specific decision or action and understand that if things had been done differently, they might have been able to avert such a crisis. That's useful to some extent, but there is a second type of 'failure' that I'd argue is an even more valuable lesson. However, unlike these huge corporate crises, these examples are much subtler, and maybe the word 'failure' is a little bit harsh. The type of example I'm referring to is when companies actively try and implement a CSR strategy, but for whatever reason, it doesn't quite have the desired effect. That is to say that consumers don't get too impressed by it, and the firm's reputation is left pretty much un-changed.

From a company's point of view, they might be tempted to conclude that their customers simply don't care about CSR and that it's not worth the amount of time and effort that they're putting into it. After all, if companies don't think that CSR is benefitting them, it'll become harder and harder to justify doing it at all. Yes, you could say that in an ideal world, CSR doesn't need to create a return on investment, but if we want business to make the world a better place, it has to be sustainable. Like I've already said, the perfect outcome is for CSR to help businesses be successful, while also helping society. The second that the scales of that balance tip in a certain direction, problems will arise. If a business just cares about society but isn't getting any benefit themselves, they won't be able to sustain their efforts. Similarly, if they only care about themselves and not society, then we'll never stray from the underlying system in which the most irresponsible companies make the most money.

Anyway, writing off CSR because a specific initiative hasn't been successful would be a premature conclusion for a company to draw. As I've highlighted with the results of my study, and that similar studies have proven, is that consumers do care about CSR. What's more, they're only caring more and more as time goes on. With this in mind, if a particular CSR strategy doesn't lead to a more positive reputation, then it's probably down to the way that the strategy was put together, rather than CSR not mat-tering to people. What I'd like to do, therefore, is look at some examples of where this has happened. By working through some companies that have just fallen short of CSR success, we'll be able to see how important all of the ideas presented in this book can be. In an attempt to favour quality over quantity, I'll focus on just three different companies, namely PepsiCo, Starbucks, and Dell. Each of these companies engage in CSR reasonably heavily, but none of them would spring to mind if I had to name some responsible companies. Let's work through them individually to see where they went wrong.

PepsiCo

More commonly referred to as just 'Pepsi', PepsiCo are undoubtedly a company that take CSR seriously. So much so that in 2017, Corporate Responsibility magazine named them as one of the world's 100 best corporate citizens. That's quite an achievement when you consider their arch nemesis, Coca-Cola, was named by Ethical Consumer as one of the 10 most unethical companies of the last 25 years. With that in mind, you'd expect Pepsi to be laughing all the way to the bank, cashing in on their newfound glowing reputation. However, this is far from the case, and the particular initiative that can shine some light on why is the Pepsi Refresh Project (PRP).

In essence, the project was simple and undeniably socially beneficial. It took the form of a nationwide community grants scheme, offering out a total of $20 million to various charities, non-profits, and social enterprises. Organisations could apply for a grant of up to $250k, and once 1000 organisations had applied, Pepsi utilised a public voting system to allocate all the money. This basic process would then repeat with another 1000 applications and so on and so on. It was at this point where it got even more clever. While members of the public could vote online, Pepsi introduced the idea of 'power votes' which could only be accessed using codes printed on the inside of all their drinks. Power votes were worth anywhere between 5 and 100 times more than a regular vote, which would obviously make a significant difference to the outcome of the money allocation. On the face of it, it sounds absolutely perfect. Thousands of great causes would receive crucial funding, and Pepsi would surely capitalise from people buying their products to unlock power votes.

On top of that, Pepsi were the main sponsors of the Super Bowl that year and focused almost exclusively on the PRP as their marketing message.

So how did it all work out? Well, people generally took to the idea really well, the initial engagement was good, and some consumers would specifically buy Pepsi to access more votes. However, by 2012, Pepsi's market share had declined so much that Diet Coke overtook them as the second best selling soft drink, leaving Pepsi in a somewhat uncomfortable third position. Not long after that, Pepsi scrapped the Refresh Project, and its legacy has mainly lived on through blog articles of CSR failures.

To try and understand why that is, we should look for evidence of the three pillars (targeting, integrating and communicating) in Pepsi's strategy. The obvious place to start is communication. Pepsi used the most valuable advertising slot in the world to push a CSR initiative, and it worked. The super bowl ad strategy was a good move, as it helped spread their message in arguably the most efficient way possible. Secondly, the voting process had a substantial social media component. With voting taking place online, Pepsi were able to speak to people on the platforms that work the best, with Facebook, Twitter and YouTube all being used intensively to connect with their socially conscious consumers. From a communication standpoint, it's hard to find any particular faults in their campaign. Granted, the super bowl advert would have cost them a lot of money, thus making it harder to achieve a return on investment, but in what was a generally weak year for super bowl advertising, it certainly wasn't the reason that this project 'failed'.

Next, let's look at integration. As I've already said, PepsiCo are a company that value CSR, they wouldn't have won so many awards if they didn't. In 2006, they introduced their 'Performance with Purpose' initiative. It was introduced by the CEO at the time, Indra Nooyi, and set out to 'ingrain' sustainability into their daily activities. It's quite impressive too, containing an environmental and a social arm, while also making sure that their products are socially responsible. Without actually working at PepsiCo, it's impossible to say how integrated CSR really is. However, I've seen more than my fair share of CSR jargon, and the more I learn about Pepsi's 'Performance with Purpose', the more convinced I am that it's not just for show.

To be honest, the awards they've won are a testament to the positive societal influence they have had over the years, and I'd be inclined to say that Pepsi's CSR is integrated at least to the point where it isn't responsible for the failure of the PRP. The problem is, most CSR related awards don't actually reward good CSR, they simply reward companies that benefit society, which I've hopefully proved is not the same thing. For the most part, whether or not CSR actually benefits the business in any way doesn't tend to be a factor in these award decisions. That's why Pepsi can be considered such a responsible business. Even though the PRP didn't actually end up boosting consumer image, it clearly was introduced with the right intention. This idea brings us nicely onto the one CSR box that PepsiCo forgot to tick, which is targeting.

The problem with the refresh project, was, in my opinion, mostly down to its lack of a commercial and industry focus. Don't get me wrong it was an incredibly altruistic social initiative, but it fell so far to the social side of the balance that Pepsi couldn't justify sustaining it.

The grants that Pepsi awarded while the project was live were spread out into six different categories; Health, Arts & Culture, Food & Shelter, The Planet, Neighbourhoods, and Education. While this was great for society as a whole, the scope was so broad that consumers couldn't conceivably believe that Pepsi were genuinely committed to tackling every one of these issues. As I demonstrated in chapter four, people will generally perceive a company to be more socially responsible if they address the specific issues that their industry creates. By not necessarily doing that, the whole program came across like a bit of a gimmick. By being completely separate from both their industry and their products, the Pepsi Refresh Project didn't resonate with consumers enough for them to buy into their social vision. Instead, it merely created a brief spike in interest before dying out.

That's why targeted CSR is so fundamental. While effective communication can help a company get noticed by the right people, creating a long-lasting positive reputation takes more than just an expensive advert. It takes an honest acceptance of the negative consequences resulting from their business, and a genuine commitment to negate them. I can't help but think if Pepsi ploughed their resources into more relevant issues such as plastic in the oceans, or recycling in general, the project may have survived much longer. Granted, the initial spike in sales may not have been as high, but the longevity of their reputation might have offset that in the long term.

Unfortunately for Pepsi, I think this oversight, albeit a seemingly minor one, was the final nail in the coffin for the PRP. While I'm in no way suggesting that either Pepsi or the Refresh Project are examples of irresponsibility, it just goes to show that unless the balance between business and societal benefits is perfectly struck, CSR cannot be truly effective.

Starbucks

Perhaps the inclusion of Starbucks will come as a surprise to anybody who keeps up with CSR related news. Starbucks have come under fierce public scrutiny multiple times for the way that they behave as an organisation. Still, you can't deny that on the face of it at least, they invest a fair amount in some forms of CSR activity. However, what is it that Starbucks does wrong? Why is it that numerous consumers actively boycott them because of how irresponsible they are? Unlike with PepsiCo, this example doesn't focus on one specific CSR initiative but instead looks at Starbucks' approach to CSR on the whole. It's easy enough to find evidence of the great things they're doing that benefit society, but for whatever reason, consumers are less than impressed.

The main box they tick is communication. Like Pepsi, Starbucks are not afraid to talk about CSR, and they're very active on social media. Their global Facebook page has over 11 million likes, and you don't have to scroll for too long before finding content that relates to inequality, LGBTQ issues and even the refugee crisis. Starbucks are quite happy to include this type of content along with the usual product-based marketing videos, and it seems to work pretty well. Most CSR related posts have an impressive amount of likes, shares, and comments (certainly enough to warrant the effort), and it makes you think that maybe everybody is jumping to conclusions and that they're not all that bad. But what about targeting?

This area is undeniably the first criteria that Starbucks don't meet very convincingly. The problem is, their entire CSR strategy is hugely fragmented. For a long time, Starbucks' main issue was pioneering Fair Trade coffee, and they did so really well. Now, however, they're spreading themselves very thin, trying to cover as many issues as possible in the hope that consumers will approve of at least some of their actions. They swing from race campaigns to Fair Trade farming to the refugee crisis, with next to no overriding ambition connecting it all. I have to stress that while you could say such an approach is admirable, it's not going to help people see Starbucks as a 'responsible company'. They'd no doubt be better off maximising the positive impact of their Fair Trade work, than try and address every problem within society.

Unless something changes, consumers will continue to see them as just another company that does a few responsible things. I know I've mentioned this distinction before, but it's an all too familiar one in the world of CSR. When I look at the strategy that Starbucks have adopted, it seems quite disorganised and frantic. There appears to be no primary direction behind what they're doing, and that manifests itself as insincerity when it comes to communicating with consumers. What Starbucks therefore need to do, is take a step back and assess their allocation of resources. If they specialised in tackling some key issues within the coffee industry, they could have a far more profound social influence, and that would start to be noticed by consumers. By spreading their resources too thin, they leave themselves effectively forced to occupy the 'reactive' boxes of the CSR activity matrix (from chapter three), meaning they'll struggle to turn their actions into a sustainable competitive advantage.

Unfortunately for Starbucks however, their problems don't end there. As we look towards the final pillar of integration, it becomes quite difficult to find any real evidence that CSR is something deeply ingrained into the identity of the company. Realistically, when CSR is part of a firm's DNA, they should be engaging in both targeted and generic activities proactively. When CSR really matters, it reverberates around the whole organisation, influencing the behaviour of all business functions, from HR to Marketing to Finance. Usually, this takes the form of a company-wide CSR programme. With PepsiCo, that was their Performance with Purpose initiative, and the earlier example of Unilever have their Sustainable Living Plan. So what do Starbucks have? Well, a few years ago, Starbucks did launch an initiative called Starbucks™ Shared Planet™. Whoever devised such a name clearly didn't understand the irony of plastering it with trademarks.

In essence, it was an initiative very similar to Plan A by M&S. It focussed predominantly on ethical sourcing as well as some recycling initiatives and volunteer work. However, while doing the necessary research for this chapter, it proved to be something that was very hard to find any information on. The only place I was able to gather any meaningful content was from the Starbucks 'Newsroom', where members of the press can go for corporate information. I think that tells you all you need to know about Starbucks' level of CSR integration and how seriously they take it. It would appear then, that Starbucks have scrapped the programme, as the custom website that used to host it now just redirects to the standard Starbucks CSR page.

What Starbucks lacks, and what the more 'successful' companies don't, is an enduring social ambition that slowly weaves itself into the company's identity. Without this, I can't help but, perhaps cynically, think that it's all just for show. Importantly though, is the fact that I'm almost definitely not alone. It's no wonder that Ethical Consumer labelled Starbucks as the most unethical coffee company in the UK in 2011.

Overall, while Starbucks no doubt have the resources to invest in CSR, and the captive audience to benefit from it, I think they lack the genuine desire to do it properly. Let's not forget that combining the three pillars or CSR may be a simple concept to comprehend, but it doesn't make it effortless to implement. For a company to manage it, they'll have to truly care about making the world a better place. What will be interesting then, is to keep an eye on Starbucks to see if there becomes a point at which they are effectively forced to take it a bit more seriously.

Dell

By this point, you might have worked out where I'm going with this. If PepsiCo failed due to a lack of targeting, Starbucks failed due to a lack of integration; then there's no prize for guessing Dell's downfall. The case of Dell is a sad one, as it's a prime example of a company doing pretty much everything right, but communicating it so poorly that they fail to benefit from it commercially. When you consider that they operate in an incredibly competitive industry, it's a shame to see such a responsible company not get the consumer recognition they deserve.

Anyway, as with the other two examples, let's go through the pillars of integration and targeting to demonstrate how it's pretty much just communication that is letting them down.

To start with targeting, Dell are ticking all the right boxes. Their initiatives primarily revolve around the IT industry and the negative impacts associated with it. For starters, Dell have an industry-leading recycling programme to tackle the issue of 'e-waste'. People can return their old products completely free of charge, and where possible, Dell strives to donate them to non-profit organisations and schools. They also collect ocean plastic and use it as packaging for several of their products.

In my opinion, without being unbelievable pedantic, Dell is right up there amongst the most responsible companies in the world, especially within the computing industry. Fortunately, I'm not the only one making such a claim. In January 2018, Dell was recognised by Ethisphere as one of the World's 100 Most Ethical Companies'. The 100 companies aren't actually ranked, but I think the fact that 2018 is the fifth consecutive year that Dell have been recognised, speaks volumes for their CSR strategy.

So what about integration? What sort of enduring social ambition does Dell have that makes all of their actions seem legitimate? Well, in 2013, Dell introduced their 'Legacy for Good' plan. The plan is a detailed set of social ambitions that they seek to achieve by 2020. They have a dedicated website for it, and it and was launched by the president of the company. More impressively, however, is how they've worked through their plan, particularly as they've reached the latter stages. After realising they were exceeding some of their targets, instead of scaling back their efforts, they altered their targets, making them even more ambitious than when they originally came up with them. It's this dedication to social responsibility that further concretes Dell's position as a global leader for CSR.

So where has it all goes wrong? Why is it that very few people would instantly think of Dell when asked to name socially responsible companies? The problem is immediately evident when you look at their communication plan.

The thing is, as Dell's share of the consumer market has gradually declined over the years, they have been forced to retreat into the 'business to business' (B2B) markets that made them so successful in the first place. That being said, as Dell themselves have admitted, the lines between businesses, especially small business, and consumers are rapidly blurring. After all, you're still dealing with people, and you're still trying to sell them products. What Dell fails to do, is connect with those people on the platforms that matter, namely social media. Their Facebook page has over 11 million likes, but their posts receive, on average, less than 10 likes and very few shares. It is quite a poor showing.

When you consider that Dawn's chick photo managed over 700,000 post likes with just over 1 million page likes, the size of Dell's failure is made even more clear. As several social media experts have noted, social media use is not just something for businesses selling to the general public, and Dell's B2B focus is certainly no excuse. The content they post is usually very dry, and product focused, with next to nothing relating to their wider corporate identity. Interestingly though, the rare few posts that do relate to their 'Legacy for Good', have nearly all received upwards of 50 or 60 likes. Granted, this is still a long way off the success that Dawn enjoyed, but it's nearly 20 times more than most of their regular posts manage.

Unfortunately, to make things even worse, the only way you can find out about the details of their CSR activity is by downloading their report. If there's one thing that I don't think I could emphasise enough, it's the ineffectiveness of CSR reports. That's not to say that companies shouldn't have them, it's just that they shouldn't be relied on for consumers to get the right information. Modern communication methods such as social media should be the platform of choice, with a detailed report then available for those that want to delve a little deeper. I'd be willing to bet that the number of people that have read it front to back is fewer than the 47 pages that it takes up. Granted, the independent website for their 'Legacy for Good' is quite easy on the eye, but it's hardly promoted on the platforms that matter. What's the point in having a beautiful website if you don't send anybody to go and look at it? It's like shouting in an empty room.

Overall, Dell's CSR strategy is sizably weakened by their poor communication of it. Maybe if they had responded quicker to the rapid growth of social media, and used it correctly, they would still be the consumer serving powerhouse they once were.

So, in PepsiCo, Starbucks and Dell, we have clear, real-life examples of where CSR has been tried but ultimately fallen short of striking that perfect balance between social and corporate prosperity. In each instance, the cause of the failure was mainly due to the company neglecting one of the three criteria for successful CSR. As I stated when introducing the criteria concept, no single one is more of less importance than the others. As the three examples show, neglecting just one of them is enough to make genuine CSR 'success' highly unlikely. I suppose some may argue that failure to communicate CSR is less of a big deal than failing to integrate it into the company, but I think such an argument would be missing the point entirely. Granted, if just looking at social benefits, communication is of less importance than the other two, because communication only really exists to benefit the company. The point I have to keep returning to, however, is that without benefiting the company, CSR can't be genuinely sustainable. If you think long term, a company that is super responsible for five years is far less advantageous than a company that is slightly less responsible, but that can last forever. Therefore, a CSR approach that benefits the business adopting it will also help society as time goes on.

However, there is one final question that I feel the need to answer. Of the three success criteria, which one, if any, is the easiest for companies to change if they need to? In short, of PepsiCo, Starbucks and Dell, who will have the most comfortable time reversing their fortunes? Perhaps the easiest way to answer this question is to start in reverse. When it comes to which criterion is the hardest to achieve, it's undoubtedly integration.

Integration is the glue that holds CSR together. Without it, both targeting and communicating CSR can still look insincere.

Although, that's not why it's the hardest to achieve. That comes as a result of the ambition associated with it. To integrate CSR, especially in a large company, there needs to be a widespread belief that it's essential, often started by the CEO and other members of senior management. This can be an incredibly frustrating process. Generally speaking, business leaders either value CSR or they don't. If they don't, it's unlikely that any business case, no matter how strong, will convince them otherwise. They may be persuaded to engage in the occasional CSR initiative, but to pioneer a new corporate identity built on social responsibility is hugely ambitious. Having said that, the converse is also true. If a leader cares about CSR, they tend to really care, and they often focus on it, at least to some extent, without much probing. A leader like Paul Polman is a prime example.

The difficulty associated with integrating CSR is therefore somewhat predetermined and depends heavily on the attitude of those in charge. Fortunately, it's likely that the era of conscious consumers will also produce an age of conscious leaders, so, in the not too distant future, such a task may not be as challenging.

Secondly is the idea of targeting. I think, for the most part, targeting is quite a straightforward process. If following the matrix that I laid out in chapter three; it would be quite easy for a company to identify how they're using their resources and whether or not they could do so more efficiently. A prime example being for a business to decide to hold back on tackling issues unrelated to their industry, in order to have a more significant effect on those that are more relevant. The only stumbling block with this criterion is ensuring that the appropriate balance is found between generic and targeted activity. While it's obviously essential to focus on the key issues, doing so at the expense of generic CSR activities could be a risky strategy in the long run. However, by understanding which generic issues matter to people, and could therefore damage reputation if overlooked, companies should be able to allocate their resources without too much trouble.

The final one, therefore, is communication. Successfully meeting this criterion is a bit of an interesting one. On the face of it, using platforms like social media to full effect and holding back on traditional reporting seems quite straightforward. However, becoming known as a genuinely engaging company can take a bit of time. With social media, companies will need to persist a little bit if they want to win over customers, as it certainly won't happen overnight. Additionally, as communication creates the risk of going viral for all the wrong reasons, successful CSR marketing relies on having already met the first two criteria. If a company's CSR strategy is appropriately targeted and integrated, communicating it will be far more painless than if they're merely trying to give off the impression that they're responsible. Therefore, while the actual practice of communicating CSR is quite simple, the requirements for maximising success combined with the extremely high risk of failure, make it something to be respected.

In short, none of the three pillars are consistently easier to implement than the others, and it's all a matter of context. Looking at these three companies however, I would say that Pepsi has the easiest task, followed by Dell, and finally Starbucks. Pepsi have the CSR philosophy and the social media presence, they just need to tackle issues that customers care about. Dell are doing all the right things, they just need to tell people about it, but Starbucks have a more fundamental issue. By not having as clear a CSR philosophy as the other two companies, they'll almost need to start from scratch. Throw in the fact that some consumers are already boycotting them, and their task becomes even more sizable.

Anyway, as these examples have hopefully shown, CSR, while conceptually straightforward, does need to be taken seriously and implemented properly. Tick all the boxes and meet the criteria and success is close to guaranteed, but cut a few corners, and it's borderline impossible.

7

Dolphins & Bananas

If you're anything like me, you can probably relate to frantically running around your house looking for something, only to find it's been embarrassing close to you all along. I've searched for sunglasses that are on my head, phones that are in my hand, and keys that are in my coat pocket. It's as if for some reason we have such a powerful trust in our self-awareness that we don't even consider searching a little closer to home. This metaphor, while admittedly tenuous, can relate quite closely to CSR. By definition, our natural instinct is to assume that CSR is simply the idea of an organisation engaging with the people that sit outside of it. This makes sense really, as when we look at the stakeholder theory of organisations, most of them are external parties. However, solely viewing CSR in this manner can be wholly inadvisable, as it may mean organisations overlook possibly one of the most important stakeholder groups that they have. Their employees.

Up until now, the vast majority of this book has focussed on customers, and how their purchasing can enable a business to achieve that much needed competitive advantage. However, it would be incomplete to suggest that socially conscious consumers hold all the cards when it comes to responsible business. Another way that firms can benefit is by ensuring they are responsible when dealing with and managing their employees. Of course, it may be tempting to look at anything to do with employees as an HR issue and not a CSR issue, but such segregation would be unwise. While many large organisations have CSR departments, that doesn't mean that other business divisions don't have their own social obligations to try and meet. While HR may be the team that actually deals with employee management, CSR can be seen as the prevailing ideology that creates the urgency to do so. The difference is perhaps even less noticeable in smaller businesses, who may not even have individual departments, but merely generalised managers who are responsible for a little bit of everything. Certainly, in these instances, CSR can't feasibly exist as separate from any other business area.

Throughout this chapter, I'm going to touch on three of the main 'HR' issues that have a legitimate CSR component. I admit that there are probably countless others that I won't mention, but the few that I will talk about will hopefully be enough to make the point that neglecting employees in a CSR strategy could be a costly error to make. The three areas I'm going to address are as follows:

1. Anti-discrimination

2. The 'other' pay gap (i.e. not the gender one)

3. Employee ownership

If you've been keeping up, you may be thinking that these types of issues could be categorised as 'generic' activities from the matrix laid out in chapter three. In which case you would be completely right. As I highlighted at the time, generic activities are simply any CSR actions that aren't specific to any given company or industry. Issues like tax avoidance could be labelled as generic, but so too could employee related ones such as the three I've mentioned above. As you may also remember from the matrix, being proactive about generic issues won't necessarily give a company a competitive advantage, but that doesn't mean they aren't worth doing. As the matrix suggests, getting these kinds of issues right could help mitigate risk and preserve a company's reputation in the long run. This is certainly true for issues like pay gaps and discrimination. If companies actively don't discriminate, consumers probably won't even realise, let alone alter their purchasing patterns accordingly. However, if a company gets found out for discriminating against members of the LGBT community, then it could be a nationwide court case. That's why, as I've implied throughout this book, CSR shouldn't be a case of just engaging in targeted activities, but finding the right balance between generic and targeted to create the biggest return for both society and the business in question.

With that in mind, let's go through the three issues I've identified and see exactly what consequences, positive or negative, they may have on a company's image and performance.

Anti-discrimination

Of the three areas I've highlighted, this is probably the one I'll talk the least about. For starters, it' pretty self-explanatory and there's quite an easy moral line for companies to draw. In essence, firms that discriminate are bad, firms that don't are good. Sadly, however, if such a statement were universally agreed upon, it wouldn't be anywhere near the pressing issue that it is. As recently as 2013/14, UK firms faced nearly 15,000 tribunals for gender discrimination, around 5,000 for disability discrimination, and approximately 3000 and 2000 for race and age discrimination respectively. Additionally, about 34% of the LGBT community in the UK choose not to disclose their sexuality at work, sometimes hiding their true self from their colleagues out of fear of ridicule, exclusion, or being overlooked for promotions. Whether their decision to do so is justifiable is almost irrelevant at this point, as ideally, employers shouldn't even make people feel that such an outcome is a possibility.

What makes discrimination such a complex issue is the sheer number of forms it can take. On the one hand, it could result in certain people not making it into senior management positions, but on the other it could be a matter or somebody not being paid the same as another colleague doing the same job, or maybe not even getting the job in the first place. In 2016, a woman named Erin McKelvey was getting a zero percent response rate from sending out her CV to potential employers. Speculating that her gender may have contributed to her struggle, she changed the name on her CV to Mack McKelvey, and her response rate increased to about 70%. In 2014, Corinne Moss-Racusin carried out a similar experiment, noting that as well as a higher response rate, the salary offered to her by employers was around $4,000 higher when they thought they were hiring a man.

The scale and scope of this issue is enormous, and I think it poses three questions that must be answered. Firstly, why is discrimination such a problem? Secondly, why is it worthwhile for businesses to address it? And finally, what is the underlying component that makes it a CSR issue?

Firstly, I think it's certainly the case that discrimination is often born out of the individual prejudice of certain managers and colleagues, rather than at an organisational level. Either that or industries that are largely dominated by one group of people may almost subconsciously discriminate against employees that don't fit the traditional mould. A prime example of this could be engineering, where only 11% of UK engineers are female, according to 2017 data.

All an organisation can therefore do is put genuine, well thought out policies and initiatives in place to try and ensure that their workforce is as diverse as the society they operate in. But, other than the moral argument, does it actually pay for firms to be anti-discriminatory? Well, while we would hope companies don't require financial incentives for not discriminating, numerous pieces of research provide some anyway. Various studies point to the idea that equal opportunities employers, the fancy phrase for companies that don't discriminate, have happier workforces on the whole. In addition, those happier workforces are more productive than others, with one study saying the productivity gain sits at around 12%. Granted, this figure may be little more than a rough estimate, but it certainly seems as though it's worth a company's effort. Combine that with the risk mitigation benefit that I've already identified, and it seems like a real no-brainer.

The issue of discrimination, and a firm's attempt to overcome it is an excellent example of CSR because it features one particular component that's worth highlighting. The thing is, while various bits of legislation exist that protect people from discrimination, it still occupies a vast grey area. As new types of contracts are introduced, and work streams such as the gig economy rise in popularity, discrimination issues become really challenging to address. As context changes over time, things that perhaps weren't considered as discriminatory before may be viewed as such now, almost giving organisation's the freedom to choose how proactive they wish to be. While companies obviously have to adhere to the law; they can effectively decide just how far they want to go to ensure that they treat every employee fairly. They can opt to do the bare minimum, or future-proof their operation, striving to set the benchmark for other companies to match. It's this ability that makes it a critical CSR issue, as it's a prime example of where organisations have to take a clear ethical stance on a broader societal problem.

The 'other' pay gap

When we think of pay gaps, we tend to think solely in terms of gender. However, as gender pay gaps come under the issue of discrimination, the pay gap I plan to talk about is something different altogether. While far less of a public talking point, the gap I'd like to discuss, and the one that I think ties in nicely with CSR, is the CEO-to-Worker pay gap. This is essentially the difference between the highest paid member of staff, usually the CEO, and the median salary for a worker in the same organisation.

Before we look at some of the startling figures that relate to this issue, it's necessary to highlight both why it's so crucial, and why it's something that falls within CSR. Realistically, CSR is all about people. It's about trying to operate in a way that doesn't negatively affect other human beings. In some cases, this link is really easy to spot, such as ensuring that child labour isn't used in manufacturing, or ensuring that workers aren't mistreated to the point that they contemplate suicide. It doesn't take a genius to acknowledge that these practices directly involve people's lives. In other cases, though, the relationship is a little bit subtler. Take tax avoidance for example. When we think about tax avoidance, we realise that it's morally questionable, but do we follow through with realising just how much it impacts other people?

A recent study estimated that the UK government miss out on up to £5.8bn in corporation tax. Straight away we can label that as a negative thing, but all too often that's where our analysis stops. Do we, for example, realise how that £5.8bn is more than the UK spent on job seeker's allowance in 2011/12? The positive contribution to society that the government could make if they collected all that tax could have a genuine and tangible effect on the lives of hundreds, maybe thousands of citizens. Alternatively, that amount of money could be used to build approximately ten new hospitals, saving thousands of lives for many years to come.

Even some of the CSR issues that seem unrelated to people have an innately human component, with environmental initiatives being a prime example. When we look at saving the environment, what we are trying to do is ensure that future generations of humans have the same opportunities as the ones we have enjoyed throughout our lives. We want our children and grandchildren to have the same resources, the same functioning eco-systems and the same quality of life. It's all based on people in some way or another. Perhaps more specifically, it's based on the equality of people. The very notion that irrespective of geographic location, gender, age or any other variable, we are all fundamentally the same, and equally important.

It is this idea that makes the CEO-Worker pay gap quite pivotal. If we want firms to be socially responsible, we are effectively asking them to treat people equally and fairly, and what better place to start than with their employees. So just how bad is this pay gap? Let's look at some examples that answer that very question.

It's probably worth pointing out that far more research has been done on this issue in the U.S. than in the UK, so most of the data will be related to American companies. However, there are still some figures for UK companies that provide the necessary level of insight.

For starters, a 2017 study highlighted that, on average, a CEO in America makes approximately 271 times the salary of the median worker. That means that they will earn in less than two days what most workers will receive in a year. That's a mind-boggling level of inequality. To put that in perspective, since 1978, CEO pay has increased by over 930%, outpacing both the stock market and the wealth of the often demonised 'richest 1%'. Looking on the bright side, the 271:1 ratio has decreased a fair bit from being 376:1 in 2000 but it is still incomparable to the 20:1 and 59:1 ratios recorded in 1965 and 1989 respectively.

In the UK, the issue is slightly less obscene, with a pay gap of 'only' 129:1 in FTSE100 companies. How can a firm truly claim to be socially responsible, and therefore believe, at least to some extent, in the idea of equality, when such dramatic pay gaps exist in their organisation? Of course, I'm not suggesting that CEOs shouldn't be paid a fair bit more than the average worker, after all, they have a much harder job and greater responsibility, but I'd like to think we can agree that 129:1 is a tad excessive.

I think it's telling though, that this pay gap is something that is gradually gaining media attention, and as a result is starting to come down. Interestingly, in the UK at least, some industries have far less of a problem with this, with technology companies leading the way with a ratio of just 27:1. Perhaps this is due to tech companies having younger, and statistically more socially progressive CEOs? If so, it certainly suggests that this is a CSR trend to watch out for, and one that may come back to bite the companies that don't try and address it.

As with discrimination, I think the reason for firms to look at this form of inequality is mainly two-fold. On the one hand, they may mitigate any future reputational risk if this ratio becomes as publically prominent as the gender pay gap. On the other hand, employees are likely to feel far more valued, and organisations will be able to foster a culture of collaboration far more easily. When everybody is treated fairly and pay exists on a much narrower spectrum, yet still representative of an individual's level of responsibility, organisations will no doubt become more collaborative and innovative. With certain innovations improving the lives of people all around the world, finding ways to promote this would be a prime example of a company making both business and societal sense.

Of course, these speculations may not have monumental positive effects, but in a future world where competition is fierce and CSR is, to some extent, the norm, these are precisely the type or marginal gains that businesses may require.

Employee ownership

While the previous two issues are somewhat specific examples of responsible approaches to employee treatment; this final one is significantly more systemic. As the title suggests, this topic relates to having a business model where the employees of an organisation are also the 'owners' or 'partners' of that organisation. A prime example, in the UK at least, is the John Lewis Partnership. For pretty much the entirety of their history, the John Lewis Partnership have adopted, and in many ways pioneered, the concept of employee ownership. Currently, all 84,000 permanent members of staff 'own' the company, and as a result, get a share of the profits that they make each year. If CSR is about establishing a connection between businesses and society, or people in general, then an employee-owned business model is as close to a perfect solution as you're likely to find. These types of business models are often confused as being non-profit or less financially motivated, but that's actually far from the truth.

In reality, profit drives the business perhaps more so than conventional companies, because every single employee stands to benefit if the company is successful. However, what makes employee-owned companies different is that they generally strive for profit with a purpose. Going right back to chapter one, I spoke about Apple's cash mountain of around $250bn. An employee-owned company would never seek to have profit for the sake of accumulating wealth because they're more interested in ensuring the company can continue for many years to come. They usually do this by reinvesting everything they make and planning for the extreme long-term rather than the short-term, something which conventional shareholders of other companies have been known to resist.

The benefits of these models make for excellent reading. Numerous studies have shown that employee engagement, survival rates and company growth are all higher amongst employee-owned firms than conventional companies. What's more, in times of economic uncertainty, employee-owned businesses usually make far fewer people redundant, which is obviously beneficial to the economy as a whole.

What appeals to me about this type of business model is the underlying sense of compromise that seems to reverberate within it. For example, the company still aims to make a profit, just not for the sake of it, choosing instead to share it and use it for something more socially beneficial than mere wealth accumulation. Again going back to chapter one, I spoke about how businesses become less responsible as their survival becomes more guaranteed. That's why small companies tend to be more tightly connected to their communities than larger ones. What employee-owned firms do is find a way to organically grow into a larger organisation, without losing that primary target of ensuring survival. You see, in a company like John Lewis, 'partners' are unable to sell their shares in the company and invest in something else. This fact means that it's in their best interest to ensure that the company continues to survive. It's a very effective way to ensure that they can never get ahead of themselves.

The good news is that these types of businesses are no longer as few and far between as they once were. Growing in number by approximately 10% each year, employee-owned organisations are the fastest growing business type in the UK. As of 2017, these types of companies employed upwards of 200,000 people and contributed to the economy with a combined turnover of around £40bn. The obvious question, therefore, is this: if an employee-owned structure is so fantastic, why isn't everybody doing it?

Firstly, a misconception exists where entrepreneurs think that they need to decide on this type of business model from the get-go. While that is a possibility, it would involve placing an enormous amount of trust on the people around you, without really having worked with them for very long. A more realistic approach is for the original business owner to adopt a conventional business model as the they grow the company and establish themselves. Then, when the entrepreneur wants to retire, they can just sell their shares of the company to the employees. It's a great way to create an employee-owned model without jumping in at the deep end and gives the original owner a nice retirement pot. For all we know, many current business owners could be planning such a transition. What we might therefore see is a considerable spike in employee-owned businesses, as the entrepreneurs from the last 20 years or so reach the point where they wish to step aside.

On the flip side of that, there are the larger companies. Companies like Apple that are already so dominant, with an infinitely complex organisational system, not to mention being listed on the stock exchange, that makes employee ownership practically impossible. I think in the coming years we will see a visible divide in the business world, with employee ownership becoming the default alternative to the more conventional business models. At this stage, it's impossible to foresee precisely how popular this structural approach may become, but given the seismic change in the value of CSR, I wouldn't be prepared to bet against anything.

However, it's perhaps necessary to note, especially with regards to the idea of employee ownership, that it isn't, nor should it be viewed as, a replacement for CSR. Instead, companies should see it as a merely credible strategy for achieving it. A company that adopts an employee-owned model will still need to meet the three criteria of targeting, integrating and communicating, in order to be successful. The only difference is that they may have a significant head start when it comes to doing so.

What I hope this chapter has done is reinforce the fundamental people-centric nature of CSR. Once we acknowledge that some sort of basic level of compassion towards other human beings lies at the heart of what it's about, the scope of it naturally expands. After all, we mustn't forget that we share over 60% of our DNA with both dolphins and bananas (which I admit sounds like a rip off of Dolce and Gabbana), so just imagine how similar we are to each other. It is this understanding that drives CSR, and it is this perspective that makes it so necessary.

On a practical level, this means employee issues transcend the remit of an HR department, and, like more commonly recognised CSR activities, become opportunities for firms to lead the way regarding positive societal influence.

8

The 94th Minute

I certainly wouldn't consider myself to be a 'betting man', but that's not necessary for the want of trying. Over the years, I've dabbled with betting on various sports, from Football to Snooker to the Bahrain Handball League. One thing that never changed though was the outcome. It seemed that regardless of the sport I was trying to bet on, I'd lose out in the most ridiculous of circumstances. A football team could be 2-0 up in the 85th minute, but they'd lose 3-2 if I had a bet on them. There's only so many 94th minute winners a person can take before realising that enough is enough.

For whatever reason though, my continued run of bad luck has not necessarily suppressed what seems like quite a strong urge to try and predict the future, an urge which I think most of us share in some way or another. Regardless of circumstances, we like to try and have some idea as to what might happen in our lives. Irrespective of whether you always try to plan ahead or not, you can't even make that decision without trying to foresee what scenarios might play out.

With that in mind, and despite my rather poor success rate, I think it might be worthwhile doing a similar exercise within the field of CSR. As I mentioned right at the start of this book, CSR is very much still in its growth phase, creeping into the mainstream as a new era of socially conscious consumers starts to influence the way firms operate. What that means, therefore, is that understanding what the future might hold is perhaps more pivotal than ever. For all we know, CSR could endure some sort of catastrophic crisis of confidence that means the general public simply stop caring for it entirely. Alternatively, the opposite extreme is possible, with CSR potentially becoming an issue of even greater importance, causing any company that ignores it to suffer from some form of corporate Armageddon.

In reality, certainly for the so-called 'near future', we're likely to observe something that sits somewhere in-between those two possibilities. Still, having some vague idea of the direction CSR is going in will no doubt help ensure that businesses and entrepreneurs are not left behind. After all, that's the situation many are currently finding themselves in since CSR has grown over the last couple of decades. In many ways, it emerged so quickly that most companies have been playing catch up ever since, with only a select few getting ahead of the game and setting the benchmarks for what businesses can achieve. I think, therefore, that if we could somehow predict, with at least some certainty, how the next few decades might play out, larger companies may be able to make a more convincing business case for CSR initiatives, and smaller companies may trust that it's something that will help with their survival and growth.

To that end, this chapter will propose my top 5 predictions surrounding CSR, and how they may change the way that businesses need to approach and value it. By nature, it is somewhat speculative, but as I go through, I hope you'll see that not one of them is so drastically unrealistic that you should discount it entirely. To make it seem less like a random outpouring of ideas, I'll introduce them in order of likelihood. While I like to think that number one will be pretty much guaranteed, number five might force you to suspend your disbelief ever so slightly.

The other thing I should also point out is that all five of my predictions are things I expect to happen between now and 2050(ish). There's no real value in going much further than that because the wider context could be so drastically different to what it is now that we could probably argue that literally anything may happen. For all we know, people in the year 3000 genuinely might live underwater, so even speculating to such a timeframe seems meaningless. 2050, however, is a bit more relatable.

Firstly, I like to think I'll be alive to see it, so that always helps, but also, any contextual changes probably won't exist beyond the parameters of our imagination. If somebody from 2050 built a time machine and came back to tell us what the future is like, the time machine would probably be the biggest surprise, if you get what I mean. Secondly though, it's far enough away that nobody will remember these predictions, saving me the humiliation for when they're embarrassingly far off the mark.

Anyway, with that short disclaimer in place, here are my 5 CSR predictions for the next 32 years.

Selling data will catch companies out

We live in a world where most things of value are invisible and intangible. The vast majority of the money in our economy, for example, is just a series of numbers on a screen. Cryptocurrencies are yet another example of this, with the dramatic rise of Bitcoin proving a similar point. In this highly digitalised environment, it's no wonder that data is becoming a more valuable asset than ever. Whether consumers are actually conscious of it or not, companies have access to vast amounts of personal information, all of which they can use for their own self-interest. The problem for consumers, however, is that the whole notion of data is so abstract in essence that it's quite difficult for us to truly grasp the scale of the problem, or even recognise that there is a problem in the first place. In reality, when I think of data, I just think about the basic information that websites like Facebook have on me. It's really easy to think that putting my date of birth into Facebook is quite a harmless act, but in the grand scheme of things, it could contribute to some pretty complex ethical dilemmas.

As you're probably well aware, the problem with data stems not from its original purpose, but from the way it is handled and collected. For now, Facebook knowing my birthday can give me a certain amount of happiness when it reminds my friends to post a little happy birthday message on my timeline. I might not necessarily read them, but it's nice that people make the effort. However, that snippet of information forms part of a much larger online profile of me. Once compiled, that 'profile' can be sold to whichever companies value it the most, allowing them to specifically target me when it comes to touting for sales. All of a sudden, the odd happy birthday message doesn't seem so innocent, or even worth it.

The numbers behind this phenomenon are staggering, with the so-called 'data broker' industry generating over \$200bn in annual revenue, a number that will no doubt continue to rise and time goes on. The issue, of course, extends far beyond social media, with everything from browsing history, bank transactions, and even battery percentage being tracked and collated into sellable products. The latter of which is actually the most creepy, as the combination of battery percentage and time until you need to charge your device can create a unique tracking ID. This ID can allow companies to collate all of your activity and search history, even if some of it was carried out using private browsing or a VPN. I can't help but feel slightly uncomfortable about this. I don't remember allowing companies to handle my data in this way, but maybe our entire generation will be punished for not actually reading the Terms & Conditions.

In essence, the issue of data is a cause for concern for two primary reasons. Firstly, we're very much entering into the unknown. At the moment, we may think that it's harmless that Facebook ads are explicitly selected for us based on our search history. We may even be tempted to say it's convenient. I would personally disagree, as it's a right pain when you're looking to buy a present for somebody, and they see hundreds of adverts for their gift when they look over your shoulder onto your Facebook feed.

However, this is the least of our concerns, and we must realise that this is just the start of how companies may use our data, and legislation may not be able to keep up. In 2013, Tesco introduced face recognition advertising in some of their petrol station express stores, allowing specific adverts to be displayed to people that match certain appearance related criteria.

As technology advances, the ways in which data is used will likely become far more refined and sophisticated. Our entire lives will become dominated by advertising, fundamentally exploiting us to part with our money for things that we don't actually need. Various articles have already speculated that the average person sees up to 4,000 adverts a day. I can only see this number increasing, and that will force companies to buy personal data to target you more successfully and stand out from the rest. Already, some companies have been fined for illegally selling data, but what good is a fine when the damage is already done? In fairness, this use of data transcends a mere advertising issue and opens up serious questions surrounding privacy. If data is allowed to be used so ruthlessly, how far away are we from a society where every move we make is being 'watched'? It's a scary thought.

Secondly, this creates an additional issue with regards to CSR. As I mentioned in an earlier chapter, companies that no longer see people as human beings, but strands of numbers on a screen, will lack the same incentive to behave responsibly. By dehumanising the consequences of an organisation's actions, the things that firms may be willing to do could take a turn for the worse. If workers are presented as just productivity ratings, at what point do working conditions become irrelevant? If customers are just strands of information, do exploitative advertising methods really matter? While it is usually the case that the larger organisations are more susceptible to these approaches, data could completely change that. As more and more data becomes available, the price of it may decrease, making it commercially viable for small and medium-sized businesses to purchase. Once this happens, even the companies that operate on a local level may slowly lose touch with the human element of the people they engage with. This dehumanisation of commerce could have a profound adverse effect on the way that organisations operate.

My future prediction, therefore, is straightforward. As the consequences of data become increasingly more severe, it will no doubt be a far greater cause for concern amongst the average consumer. As a result, it could soon be one of the key selling points for an organisation looking to gain a responsible reputation. In the same way that some companies currently claim they don't test on animals, claiming that they don't buy or sell data might be just as meaningful in the business world of the future.

'Human-made' will become the new hand-made

No matter how quickly the world changes, there is always a little part of us that clings to some form of nostalgia. Towards the end of 2016 for example, more money was spent on vinyl records than on digital song downloads. Yes, there could just be a growing hipster population, but I'm sure that every so often, we like to remember just how simple things once were. We can make a similar observation when looking at the market for handmade goods. In our quest to be a bit more individual, we're realising that handmade products can make us feel better than buying one of the many identical items rolling off a commercialised production line. That's not to say we necessarily want to make the things ourselves though, and the rise of websites like Etsy shows that we're still happy to purchase the 'stuff' we think we need. All that's changed perhaps is that many of us want to buy things with a bit more intrinsic meaning than before. We want to be able just to know that at some point, a skilled individual spent a certain amount of time producing the very thing we've decided to buy.

With this in mind, how often do we see companies advertising that their products are handmade? It's basically a buzzword for making something 50% more expensive, without putting anybody off. This idea of something being handmade is a great selling point for a lot of companies, but this prediction will discuss that such a phrase may soon be a thing of the past.

Production methods are rapidly increasing in potential. In today's world, products can be made unbelievably efficiently to a very high standard with numerous different variants and specifications. However, what started out as clever machines giving humans a helping hand, is rapidly becoming a matter of robots replacing humans entirely. What was once a big heap of metal with a few mechanical arms is now far more humanised, with hi-tech robotics being given an artificial intelligence that isn't far away from matching, or even surpassing, the human brain. How then, will this effect CSR?

For starters, it's necessary to mention that straight away, automation is a CSR issue. If companies choose to automate all of their processes, it is likely that jobs will suffer. One such estimate is that in the U.S. alone, 73 million jobs may be lost due to automation by 2030. Sure, automation might create some high skilled jobs for those that can maintain and program these machines, but the low skilled jobs available will no doubt decrease. We cannot ignore the effect this could have on wider society, as it creates a genuine issue that we need to address. If the only jobs that get replaced, at least to start with, are the low paying ones, how will that affect inequality? Those people who already represent the poorest in society will no doubt get poorer, while the ones with higher skills, and most likely higher pay, will probably be okay. Now, if we lived in a world where everybody had the same access to the same level of education and job opportunities, it could be argued that such an economic divide is reasonable. However, considering that such a meritocracy doesn't, and probably never will, exist, such inequality is surely undesirable.

As with buying and selling data then, the issue of automation will also present businesses with an opportunity to behave more responsibly. Consumers may start to demand that companies are creating a sufficient number of jobs, and getting the automation balance right could be a valuable CSR strategy. That's not to say that companies will ever be forced to avoid automation entirely. Not only would that be a certain backward step, but it also wouldn't be economically viable. What I can see happening though, is companies choosing to publicise just how much of the production process involves humans, and how many high quality jobs they are responsible for creating. In the same way that a handmade product from Etsy makes us a bit happier as consumers, it doesn't seem inconceivable that we will get a similar feeling when buying from companies that haven't replaced all their workers with robots. Providing that the price difference isn't utterly ridiculous, I can see the issue of automation becoming deeply important to a lot of people, and the idea of a product being 'human-made' may one day actually mean something.

There will be a near-universal CSR rating system

I've spoken a lot in this book about corporate image and how consumers use their perception of firms to decide what they spend their money on. If they view a company as socially responsible, the data shows they may be more inclined to buy from them. The underlying issue with this, however, is that it all rests on perception. In theory, companies that are socially responsible might not be seen to be, while companies that aren't might just be better at selling themselves. I tried to address this issue by looking at the importance of things like integration and communication when it comes to brand image, but ultimately the problem still exists in some way or another.

Additionally, as CSR becomes essential for organisations, the number of ways in which consumers will be able to compare firms could reduce. After all, consumers, for the time being at least, see CSR as something that is entirely black and white. Firms are either responsible, or they're not. The various shades in-between are effectively irrelevant when it comes to purchasing behaviour. However, as we know from observing certain organisations, this is quite far from the truth. The more we learn about the actual CSR strategy of particular firms, the more we realise how it must exist on a spectrum. We can start to view a company like Debenhams as more responsible than Primark, but not as responsible as M&S. The idea of relativity is, from a competitive advantage standpoint, deeply ingrained in CSR.

With this in mind, consumers would no doubt benefit from a system or mechanism that effectively compares all organisation against one another. I mentioned right at the start of this book that measuring CSR is inherently difficult, and no universal measuring system currently exists. However, that's not to say that people aren't trying to create one. At the moment, various institutions have attempted to pioneer a numerical CSR index that produces a 'score' for every organisation, but no one approach has proved conclusive enough to prevail. This is entirely understandable, as evaluating the overall level of responsibility of an organisation is incredibly ambitious. Firstly, how would you even acquire the necessary information to truly understand how a company operates? This would be especially difficult for larger organisations, whose activities are spread out all around the globe. Secondly, even if you could do this, how would you go about assigning any sort of comparable value to individual issues? For example, if a company was environmentally friendly, but didn't pay their taxes, how can you conceivably say that one of those actions outweighs the other?

However, despite the apparent difficulties, I genuinely think that over the next few decades, somebody will pretty much manage it. In doing so, they will create a platform that provides companies with a CSR score, that socially conscious consumers can use to distinguish between companies. Of course, it's highly unlikely that every company will be featured, but certainly enough to be of use to prospective customers.

More specifically, I think that Ethical Consumer Magazine currently has the type of ranking system that probably comes the closest to what this future platform may look like. What they do, rather cleverly, is assign companies a score based on various criteria. In short, they've scored companies based on five categories; Environment, Animals, People, Politics and Product Sustainability. They have then collated these scores to create an overall ranking, but their method allows consumers to adjust sliders to weight the issues that matter the most to them. In the mobile phone market, with the five categories equally weighted, the iPhone scores a relatively sub-par 8/20. However, if I give Environment a heightened weighting, the score drops to 6.5. Similarly, if I decide that the People category is most important to me, their rating falls to 4.5, and the ranking of all the companies changes once more.

It is only this sort of system that can overcome the issue of trying to objectively state which issues are more important than others. By letting consumers weight issues depending on their personal values, each individual will discover the most responsible company that aligns with their values. I can see an enormous amount of potential in this type of system, and I think it just needs more resources behind it to gain the widespread acknowledgement that it deserves.

CSR won't exist (but in a good way)

I'll be first to admit that the title of this prediction is somewhat provocative. CSR as a concept won't necessarily cease to exist, but what it essentially means to organisations could change to the point where that is effectively what happens. Already, as CSR has grown into prominence, the practical essence of it within organisations has started to change. To best explain this, I think it can be broken down into three distinct phases. I believe we are currently in the second one, and it's the third and final one that forms the basis of this prediction.

Firstly, we had the introduction of the traditional CSR team. As CSR became something that businesses had to take seriously, many large organisations set up as CSR team to effectively deal with the whole 'responsibility thing' so that everybody else could get on with business as usual. During this stage, a company's CSR department would entirely manage all of the CSR related activities, often resulting in them looking somewhat detached or fragmented from a consumer's perspective. For smaller businesses, this stage was characterised by the odd token gesture, trying to show the world that they weren't all that bad. During this period, such an approach wasn't particularly harmful to businesses, because consumers were just interested in knowing that firms were doing something vaguely positive. It didn't necessarily matter how they did it.

Then came the slightly more complicated second phase that I think we're currently going through. In larger organisations, CSR departments are still very much required, but the scope of their role has expanded. As CSR has started to incorporate other functions, from HR to Marketing, a CSR team are no longer the sole creators of responsibility, but the mediators. In most organisations, a significant portion of the CSR team's job will be to work with other areas of the business, encouraging them to adopt specific methods of doing things that will boost the company's image. While the CSR department will still create the overarching strategy; they will heavily rely on other business areas to roll it out, recognising that broader integration is necessary for any real progress to be made. For smaller companies, this phase may mark the start of a more strategic view of social responsibility, slowly weaving it into their Marketing and Supply Chain practices. Importantly, this phase has mostly come about due to the changing attitudes amongst consumers. At this point, it's clear that CSR isn't a passing fad, and it's something that companies must take seriously and integrate into their corporate identity.

The third phase then, and the one that may be a couple of decades away, is the dismantlement of CSR teams in general. If we reach a point where consumers value responsibility so highly, then it will naturally become ingrained in how each business area operates. Marketing teams won't need to be convinced to release CSR content because it will become an accepted form of marketing. HR won't need a CSR team trying to introduce volunteering programs because it will become a logical part of the work that HR do. On a smaller level, small and medium-sized businesses may reach a point where they don't consciously realise that they're engaging in CSR because they're simply reacting to the main views of their target market. That's exactly the sort of future I can imagine for CSR.

So, perhaps my chosen title wasn't entirely accurate. It's not that the concept of companies benefiting society will become less important, it's that it will become such a fundamental function of business that naming and labelling it would be unnecessary.

The time frame in which this transition might happen is pretty unknown. Numerous factors could affect it, and once again it's all due to how consumers value CSR in general. While part of me worries that I'll be out of a job if it happens too soon, the more altruistic part of me appreciates that it's probably a case of the sooner, the better. As soon as businesses see meeting societal obligations as an inherent part of operating, then the power that they hold for positive change can be harnessed.

One of the biggest companies in the world will fail

I remember at the start of this chapter I said that these five predictions would be in order of likelihood, with the first being the most likely and the fifth being the most unlikely. While I believe I have done that, I can't help but think that not one of these predictions is too unrealistic. Even this one.

In business, one thing we do know is that practically nothing is guaranteed. Things may seem entirely certain, but with so many influencing factors, literally anything is possible. Perhaps that's why I think this prediction isn't as far fetched as I first made out. In short, I believe that one of the world's biggest companies that exists today will not exist by 2050. By 'world's biggest', I'm not necessarily talking about companies like Apple or Amazon, but maybe the next tier down. Perhaps one of the companies that operate on a global level and are household names in most places, but isn't in the world's top 10.

After all, we've seen similar things happen to big companies in the past. Look at the mobile phone industry as a prime example. 20 years ago, Nokia was comfortably dominating the mobile phone scene, with legendary handsets such as the 1100 and 1110 still ranked as the best selling mobile phones of all time, each with 250 million units sold. However, fast forward ten years and

Nokia massively failed to keep up with the smartphone revolution, resulting in their market share rapidly plummeting until they were effectively forced to sell to Microsoft in 2014. Fortunately for diehard Nokia lovers, they've enjoyed a bit of a resurgence, and they certainly look to be on the up in the mobile phone market. In 2017 they introduced a new version of their beloved 3310 phone, the demand for which was so high that Nokia couldn't actually fulfil it. However, Nokia's resurgence is a rarity, and you only need to look at the downfall of a similar company, BlackBerry, to see that. Amazingly, BlackBerry phones still exist, but they've radically transformed into a software company just to stay afloat. It's a pretty desperate time.

While these two companies may now be heading in different directions; there is one thing that they both have in common. They lost out big time as a result of ignoring a pivotal trend. When Apple completely changed the game in 2007 with the original iPhone, most companies were quick to realise that the entire mobile phone concept was about to change, frantically upping their R&D efforts to catch up. Nokia and BlackBerry were a bit more stubborn, and they certainly paid the price.

Over the next few decades, I think some large companies may meet a similar fate, with the trend this time being the rise of CSR. As the idea of social responsibility continues to gain traction, there will almost definitely be some companies that make a conscious effort to stick to what they know best. Granted, the transition might be slower than the smartphone revolution, but I'm sure that they'll be at least one company that gets left behind. It would be little more than blind guessing if I were to try and suggest which specific industry this company might belong to, as it's impossible to tell. I would, however, imagine that it will be an industry that already takes CSR quite seriously, such as clothing or automotive. If a car company doesn't make the switch to alternative fuels, for example, some of the fines that they may receive are crippling. Within the EU, car companies have quite tough targets to hit, and those who produce larger, less environmentally friendly vehicles might have to get their act together. Similarly, clothing companies are already getting a lot of backlash for the way they produce and market their products. Give it a decade or two and a disaster like the Primark factory collapse could be enough to sink a company for good.

So, if those are my five predictions for the future of CSR, what could be the 94th-minute winner that ruins my bet? What factors could prevent any of these predictions from coming true?

Of course, when trying to predict what might happen over the next three decades, countless variables could play a vital part. There are two, however, that I think may have the most significant chance at derailing my vision; the economy and the political landscape.

Looking at the economy, it's not difficult to see how it may affect the future of CSR as a concept. As I've already stated a couple of times, most research in the field of CSR focusses on what consumers intend to do and how they say they'll behave. The conclusion of this research can, therefore, be very different to how they actually act. The difference between intention and actual behaviour increases wildly in times of economic downturns and recessions. After all, CSR, for the time being, does come at some cost. The companies that are the most irresponsible will probably be able to sell products at a lower price, which could be a far greater temptation during a recession. Naturally, when money isn't exactly tight, consumers are more likely to buy from socially responsible companies, but that premium may soon go out the window if people are living paycheck to paycheck. Regardless of how much they value social responsibility, people may be financially unable to do anything about it. What's more, our economy is currently going through some pretty significant changes. With the effects of things like Brexit still mostly unfelt, we're pretty much waiting for the economy to react. While everything could turn out okay, it's still very much unknown, and it would be unwise to write off the possibility of economic decline.

That leads me quite nicely to the other major player when it comes to CSR, which is the political landscape. Generally speaking, CSR doesn't necessarily align with a specific political stance. However, that's not to say that they aren't any political movements that might alter its future. Generally speaking, the political landscape in many countries is becoming increasingly divided, and a return to various forms of nationalism and patriotic identity is currently taking hold in many countries. This phenomenon is not inherently harmful, and it's not my intention to discuss the pros and cons of such a movement, but it could well have an effect of the success of CSR as an idea. As I talked about in the previous chapter, a big part of CSR is the human element, the belief that everybody deserves to be treated fairly and equally. After all, that's why we care when companies use child labour, or when working conditions in Bangladesh are so unethical. Now, while it is certainly not a guarantee, is it not possible that these movements could create, at least in part, an 'us vs them' mentality that undermines such unconditional equality? Is it possible that we could feel less connected to global issues provided that our own country is benefitting? As I said, it's no guarantee, but I think it's possible. Admittedly, the younger generation largely oppose these political movements, so while this effect might not take hold in the long run, it's impossible to rule out entirely.

The second political issue relates to the role of governments. Different governments will naturally have different views and policy suggestions for tackling specific issues. Therefore, the way that governments approach these matters and, more importantly, position them to the public, could have a profound effect on how consumers think. For example, parties that provide more financial incentives to social enterprises and small business could speed up the adoption of CSR, whilst those that don't clamp down on tax evasion, might make slow it down.

One thing that I honestly do believe, however, is that the only thing that can genuinely change is not whether or not CSR becomes more important, but the rate at which it does so. Naturally, external influences might slow down its growth, but I can't see them reversing it entirely, and it's for that reason that I think, some day at least, these five predictions might just come true.

9

Carnival

As I've been writing this book, numerous people have asked me what it's about. I naturally tell them that it's about corporate social responsibility, but most of the time such a snappy answer isn't particularly valuable. For the most part, people don't feel the need to learn the 'proper' business names for things. While I've said that consumers are starting to value CSR, that doesn't necessarily mean that they all know the acronym. All it means is that they're starting to demand that businesses have a more positive effect on society. The official term for such a concept is completely irrelevant. As a result of this, my succinct answer to the earlier question is usually met with a sort of vacant expression. It's not until I try and summarise what CSR actually is that I'm awarded a subtle approving nod as if to suggest that it's something worth writing about.

That's the thing that continues to strike me with CSR. Yes, there's a lot of business jargon associated with it, and it's become a bit of a buzzword, but at its heart, I like to think it's a no-brainer. The idea that companies should be a force for good in society is something that I'm sure everybody pretty much agrees with on some fundamental level. The only thing up for debate, I suppose, is what people think companies must do to be given that accolade. In the eyes of some, just making money is all that is important, because of the repercussions on the national, and even global, economy. Additionally, profitable businesses are likely to employ, and continue to employ, a number of people, which is also socially beneficial. I think it's worth highlighting that I don't in any way disagree with this viewpoint. I don't think businesses are inherently evil and of course, if they don't survive then there's no possibility of being socially beneficial anyway, so financial performance is clearly necessary. The main point I've tried to put across throughout this book, however, is that businesses have lost their way slightly. Our system has slowly emerged to reward profit regardless of social cost and punish profit with a purpose.

Irrespective of business size, it has long since been the case that ruthless profit maximisation, no matter how irresponsible, is the only way for companies to become truly successful. Sure, there are exceptions, and I've mentioned some of them throughout the previous chapters, but generally speaking, being 'good' didn't really pay off in the long run. In such a system, it would be quite naïve to simply suggest that firms have to suddenly spend loads of money on CSR. Yes, they might make the world a slightly better place, but they wouldn't survive long enough for any meaningful change to occur. Fortunately, the business landscape has started to change to a point where firms no longer need to make such a moral sacrifice in order to achieve commercial 'success'. As technology has brought us far closer to the lives of people all around the world, the future generations of consumers are viewing things fundamentally differently to their predecessors. It's from the perspective of these people that the criterion for being a socially beneficial company is far more than just making money.

However, just because consumers are more vocal about social issues, doesn't, on its own, change anything. It's only when this base level of activism starts to affect purchasing behaviour that the whole system turns upside down. You see, not only are consumers starting to genuinely care about wider society, but they also have the means required to hold firms accountable. As I discussed in chapter five, the birth of social media has not just raised awareness of specific issues but provided the platform with which ordinary people can come together to effectively ruin a firm's reputation.

Unfortunately, I was made aware of an example of this just a couple of weeks ago, after the school shooting that took place in Stoneman Douglas High School, Florida. As is the case after every other school shooting, a phrase that in itself should never have to be used, the story morphed into a wider debate on gun control. Being such a polarising topic, gun control has never really been addressed in the way that millions of people think it should be, which is why nothing hugely significant has ever been done about it. However, in the weeks following the shooting, students from the Stoneman Douglas school launched what has quickly become an international movement. Organising marches in countless cities and states, the students have appeared on talk shows and dominated social media, promoting their cause. They have stood up to Senators, spoken out about the President, and put enormous pressure on the National Rifle Association (NRA).

The NRA is one of the most powerful institutions in America, donating millions of dollars to political campaigns, and proving too mighty for any activists to ever weaken. Until now. Following the work of the Stoneman Douglas students, many multinational companies have severed ties with the NRA, refusing to give their members the discounts they have enjoyed for so many years. These companies include car rental services like Enterprise and Hertz, as well as airlines such as Delta and United.

What we can clearly observe here is exactly how powerful this next generation are, and how invested they are in social issues. These students are only 16 and 17, and yet they have publicised a social issue so effectively, that huge companies have altered their behaviour as a result. This is exactly the point I've been making in this book. People are more socially conscious than ever, and social media gives them the platform to turn their passion into power.

In a way then, when asked what this book is about, I don't think it would necessarily be incorrect to say it's all about power, and what companies must do to cope with the fact it's changing hands. I don't think it's an over-exaggeration to state that corporate power has, in many cases, proved so substantial, that even national governments can't handle and contain it. In the case of the NRA, the current U.S. government was literally funded by it, and may not be in place without their contributions. Moving away from the U.S., even institutions like the EU have limited control when dealing with businesses that span multiple continents. You only need to look at the problem of tax avoidance for this point to be proven. It is almost solely this power that has allowed companies to engage in such irresponsible business practices for so long. When they had nobody to effectively answer to, who could genuinely have stopped them? When consumers were none the wiser about their production methods, how would companies ever lose out? It is this power that has been lost, or handed back, to consumers. As with the case of the Stoneman Douglas students, when people are given the right tools, they are able to collectively influence the behaviour of even the largest organisations, something that very few governments have ever managed to do.

I think it would be unwise to underestimate just how seismic this shift has been, and yet it's very much still a work in progress. That's why I think writing this book has been a worthwhile exercise. We're at a point in time where it's too late to deny that CSR is important, but it's not too late for companies to do something about it. It's a rather convenient sweet spot to find ourselves in, but it won't last forever. As I mentioned in the previous chapter, I truly believe that some companies will be left behind after this 'responsibility revolution', and it'll be those that are yet to start taking it seriously.

I do of course understand why firms may approach the topic of CSR with some degree of caution. Because it's still a growing trend, the myth that CSR just reduces profitability has not yet been completely dispelled on a practical level. I think the general mindset is still that CSR is just another cost that companies have to deal with, and that any form of return on investment is, for the time being, unattainable. Perhaps many companies are holding out until such a definite return on investment exists. My argument, however, is that by then it will be too late. The thing is, and this is something I've tried very hard to propose in this book, is that even now, some form of return on investment is possible, it just requires a particular approach.

CSR isn't, and probably never will be, something that firms can quickly throw money at to boost their brand image. To think of it in such terms would be to underestimate the socially conscious consumer and their ability to hold firms accountable.

As with any business function, CSR needs to be carried out strategically and deliberately, and it's only then that society will be any better off. Remember, for businesses to be a real force for good in the world, they must strike a balance between commercial and societal benefits. If the societal benefits outweigh the business benefits, then it's merely philanthropy. Don't get me wrong, philanthropy is great, but as I've mentioned, it's not much use if it doesn't last. The Pepsi Refresh Project from chapter seven is a prime example of this. There's no doubt that society benefitted from the initiative, but Pepsi didn't, and it caused them to abandon it. I think as a society we can set the benchmark a little bit higher than a series of short-term philanthropic projects that quickly get abandoned by the companies who pioneer them.

However, it's equally important to emphasise that the other side of the balance is just as harmful. If the business benefits of CSR outweigh the societal ones, then it's little more than propaganda, or 'virtue signalling'. Again, this kind of approach underestimates the power that consumers now have. In an age where information is so accessible, and transparency is unavoidable, it's easier than ever for consumers to find out if companies actually are as good as they say they are.

I think perhaps this is the most accurate answer for what this book is about. Yes, it's about CSR, but I like to think it goes beyond that. It's not just about whether companies have social obligations, but how they can efficiently meet them. It's not just about how consumers are becoming socially conscious, but how firms can engage with them. It's all about achieving the elusive 'win-win' situation. What the previous chapters have attempted to do is put forward a genuine method that companies can use to strike this balance between business and societal benefits. Such pragmatism is undeniably necessary, as CSR has sometimes proved to be more of an academic construct than a useful business function. Intellectually debating the specifics of what is 'right' and 'wrong' might make for an interesting spectacle, but it doesn't provide businesses with the necessary guidance to make CSR work in the real world. In the same way that basic frameworks for things like Marketing and HR exist, CSR requires the same amount of respect, and it is only the firms that give it this respect that will come out on top.

I very much like to think that the framework I've put forward is a simple one, as it just relies on companies ensuring their activities meet three logical criteria. The successful firm of the future will make sure that their CSR is targeted. Pet projects and token gestures won't cut it in the years to come, and companies will be expected to tackle the issues that they're the most to blame for. It's no good for a wood furniture company to help the homeless if they haven't done anything about the trees they're destroying. Firms will need to get their own house in order before they can extend their efforts to other social issues. In addition, firms will also be expected to approach all of the generic activities responsibly. Granted, they might not be able to turn such actions into a competitive advantage, but it will keep them from being the victim of the next viral smear campaign.

Secondly, firms will need to integrate their efforts into their corporate DNA. Even if their activities are strategically selected, a company will have trouble convincing the public of their altruism if it doesn't go a bit further than the initiatives they choose to launch. The occasional project will mean far less to consumers than the core values of an organisation, and it is these companies that will reap the rewards of a positive image. It's also worth highlighting the long-term component of CSR integration. The successful companies of the future will no doubt look further ahead than the next fiscal year. This is something we're already seeing happen. Dell set a 2020 target back in 2013, M&S have a 2025 ambition, and Toyota have an environmental mission stretching all the way to 2050. It is only by thinking of the future that companies can ensure that they survive it.

Finally, I looked at communication. Providing a company has already taken the previous two criteria seriously, communication is what enables them to be rewarded for their efforts. By engaging with consumers, CSR can become the selling point that companies need it to be, and the balance between business and society can finally be struck. However, that's not to say it's easy, and CSR activities must still be communicated appropriately. CSR reports must exist primarily for the press and corporate partners, while social media will need to become the home of a company's altruism. Those that utilise it efficiently will have no problem attracting their customers, with companies like Dawn a case in point. On the flip side, those who get it wrong may never get the recognition they deserve, perhaps restricting their ability to sustain all their hard work.

Those that meet all three of these criteria will become a true force for good in the world. They will raise the benchmark for what businesses can achieve, and they will continually push the world to be a better place. Those that don't will be left behind, wondering if their last-ditch attempts were all a bit too little too late. I like to think that maybe the business world in 100 years' time will be noticeably different than our current one. The idea that business and commerce was once in anyway socially damaging may hopefully one day seem absurd. Perhaps it's naïve, and maybe it's optimistic, but it's not impossible.

All of the evidence points to the fact that this is the path we are currently on. Already, socially responsible companies are growing faster than ever, and out surviving their conventional counterparts. There are too many encouraging examples to name, but one thing that is abundantly clear is that this is no passing fad. As I speculated in the last chapter, it's possible that one day nobody will need to know what CSR stands for, because it won't need to even be questioned. Perhaps nobody will need to write any more books on it, or propose new theories because it will become synonymous with what business really means to people.

I'd like to end on a story. In many ancient tribal communities, a feast would be held towards the end of each winter to prepare for a period of fasting before they replenished their food supplies in the spring. The word for this type of feast was called a 'carnival'. Stemming from Latin, the word carnival can be translated as 'farewell to meat' as if these people were enjoying their final meal before an uncertain period of starvation. Traditionally, these tribes would all have hierarchies, and they would usually distribute food in accordance with those established power systems. Those at the top would eat first and eat the most before the remains gradually filtered down the pecking order. During the carnival, however, these norms were abolished. The so-called societal rulebook would be ripped up, and everybody would eat together, as equals. During the carnival, power didn't belong to the few, but to the many.

I think the business world is witnessing a similar movement. The companies that traditionally held power are handing it back to the majority, paving the way for equality to prevail. The idea that every so often, something can happen that challenges basic conventions is a powerful one, but it's something that we can clearly observe if we look for it. As consumers become more in tune with social issues, they have effectively started to rewrite the conventional business rulebook, and businesses must learn to deal with it effectively.

In essence, CSR is the world's corporate carnival, but unlike the tribal feast, I'm pretty sure it's here to stay.

So let's make the most of it.

Notes

Abbott, W.F. and Monsen, R.J. (1979) On the measurement of corporate social responsibility: Self-reported disclosures as a method of measuring corporate social involvement. *Academy of management journal,* 22(3), pp.501-515.

Alley, T.R. (1982) Competition theory, evolution, and the concept of an ecological niche. *Acta Biotheoretica,* 31(3), pp.165-179.

Alexander, R, D. and Arbor, A. (1990) *How Did Humans Evolve?* Available at: https://deepblue.lib.umich.edu/bitstream/handle/2027.42/57178/SpecPub_001.pdf?seq uen (Accessed: 4 January 2018)

Arntz, M., Gregory, T. and Zierahn, U. (2016) The risk of automation for jobs in OECD countries: A comparative analysis. *OECD Social, Employment, and Migration Working Papers,* (189), p.0_1

Ball, J., HAddou, L., and Leigh, D. (2014) *Nando's using secretive tax haven trust to avoid inheritance tax bills.* Available at: https://www.theguardian.com/business/2014/jul/10/nandos-using-secretive-tax-haven-trust-avoid-inheritance-tax-bills (Accessed: 10 February 2018)

Baron, D.P. (2001) Private politics, corporate social responsibility, and integrated strategy. *Journal of Economics & Management Strategy,* 10(1), pp.7-45.

BBC (2013) *Rana Plaza collapse: Primark extends payments to victims.* Available at: http://www.bbc.co.uk/news/business-24646942 (Accessed: 21 January 2018)

Bessen, J.E. (2016) How computer automation affects occupations: Technology, jobs, and skills.

Blau, F.D. (2016) Gender, inequality, and wages. *OUP Catalogue.*

Buchanan, T. (2015) Aggressive priming online: Facebook adverts can prime aggressive cognitions. *Computers in human behavior,* 48, pp.323-330.

Budd, N., Breakwell, A., Liu, M.X. and Schleper, C. (2015) The RIM BlackBerry PlayBook Disaster: B2B or B2C?. *Journal of Business Cases and Applications,* 13, p.1.

Butler, S. (2013) *Plan A integral to the rebirth of Marks & Spencer, says CEO.* Available at: https://www.theguardian.com/business/2013/jul/07/plan-a-integral-rebirth-marks-spencer (Accessed: 13 February 2018)

Bounds, A (2017) *Number of UK start-ups rises to new record.* Available at: https://www.ft.com/content/cb56d86c-88d6-11e7-afd2-74b8ecd34d3b (Accessed: 6 January 2018)

Carroll, A.B. (1991) The pyramid of corporate social responsibility: Toward the moral management of organizational stakeholders. *Business horizons,* 34(4), pp.39-48.

Cascio, W. (2018) *Managing human resources.* McGraw-Hill Education.

Cawsey, T. and Rowley, J. (2016) Social media brand building strategies in B2B companies. *Marketing Intelligence & Planning,* 34(6), pp.754-776.

Clive, M (2011) *Ethical Consumer Names Starbucks UK's Worst Coffee Chain.* Available at: http://www.greenbusinessnetwork.org/ethical-consumer-names-starbucks-worst-coffee-chain-in-uk/ (Accessed: 17 February 2018)

Colgan, F. (2016) LGBT company network groups in the UK: Tackling opportunities and complexities in the workplace. *Sexual orientation and transgender issues in organizations* (pp. 525-538). Springer, Cham.

Connelly, B.L., Haynes, K.T., Tihanyi, L., Gamache, D.L. and Devers, C.E. (2016) Minding the gap: Antecedents and consequences of top management-to-worker pay dispersion. *Journal of Management,* 42(4), pp.862-885.

Crain, M. (2018) The limits of transparency: Data brokers and commodification. *New Media & Society,* 20(1), pp.88-104.

Davidson, P. (2017) *Automation could kill 73 million U.S. jobs by 2030.* Available at: https://www.usatoday.com/story/money/2017/11/29/automation-could-kill-73-million-u-s-jobs-2030/899878001/ (Accessed: 16 February 2018)

Dahlsrud, A. (2008) How corporate social responsibility is defined: an analysis of 37 definitions. *Corporate social responsibility and environmental management,* 15(1), pp.1-13.

Dawn (2016) *Dawn Helps Save Wildlife. That's because Dawn is tough on grease, yet gentle on feathers.* Available at: https://www.facebook.com/dawn/photos/a.105151821819.104420.92462956819/10153 359126261820/ (Accessed: 12 February 2018)

Dawn (2018) *Dawn – Helping Save Wildlife for Over 20 Years.* Available at: https://dawn-dish.com/en-us/dawn-saves-wildlife/history (Accessed: 12 February 2018)

Di Domenico, M., Haugh, H. and Tracey, P. (2010) Social bricolage: Theorizing social value creation in social enterprises. *Entrepreneurship theory and practice,* 34(4), pp.681-703.

Diep, F. (2015) *8,000 Years Ago, 17 Women Reproduced For Every One Man.* Available at: https://psmag.com/environment/17-to-1-reproductive-success (Accessed: 5 January 2018)

Dell (2017) *An annual update on our 2020 Legacy of Good Plan.* Available at: http://i.dell.com/sites/doccontent/corporate/corp-comm/en/Documents/fy17-cr-report.pdf (Accessed: 6 February 2018)

Donnelly, G. (2017) *Top CEOs Make More in Two Days Than An Average Employee Does in One Year.* Available at: http://fortune.com/2017/07/20/ceo-pay-ratio-2016/ (Accessed: 20 February 2018)

Doz, Y. and Wilson, K. (2017) *Ringtone: Exploring the Rise and Fall of Nokia in Mobile Phones.* Oxford University Press.

Dyreng, S.D., Hoopes, J.L. and Wilde, J.H. (2016) Public pressure and corporate tax behavior. *Journal of Accounting Research,* 54(1), pp.147-186.

Ethical Consumer (2014) *Our readers vote vote for the most and least ethical companies.* Available at: http://www.ethicalconsumer.org/aboutus/ethicalconsumerat25/thebestandworstofthela st25years.aspx (Accessed: 23 February 2018)

Freeman, R.E., (1994) The politics of stakeholder theory: Some future directions. *Business ethics quarterly,* pp.409-421.

Friedman, M. (2007) The social responsibility of business is to increase its profits. *Corporate ethics and corporate governance* pp. 173-178. Springer, Berlin, Heidelberg.

Gallicano, T.D. (2011) A critical analysis of greenwashing claims. Public Relations Journal, 5(3), pp.1-21.

Gurman, M. and Webb, A. (2018) *Apple, Returning Overseas Cash, to Pay $38 Billion Tax Bill.* Available at: https://www.bloomberg.com/news/articles/2018-01-17/apple-expects-38-billion-tax-bill-on-overseas-repatriated-cash (Accessed: 18 January 2018)

Harkless, G. (2014) *20+ Entrepreneurs Explain Why They Started Their Businesses.* Available at: https://hear.ceoblognation.com/2014/04/18/20-entrepreneurs-explain-started-businesses/ (Accessed: 9 January 2018)

Hawkin, P. (1993) *The ecology of commerce.* New York: HarperBusiness.

Hendricks, D. (2014) *5 Successful Companies That Didn't Make a Dollar for 5 Years.* Available at: https://www.inc.com/drew-hendricks/5-successful-companies-that-didn-8217-t-make-a-dollar-for-5-years.html (Accessed: 2 February 2018)

Hollender, J. and Breen, B. (2010) *The responsibility revolution: How the next generation of businesses will win.* John Wiley & Sons.

Hughes, R. (2018) *Florida school shooting: Where do US protests go from here?* Available at: http://www.bbc.co.uk/news/world-us-canada-43119205 (Accessed: 25 February 2018)

Johnson, D. (2017) *Oxfam: Ten Multinational Corporations Control Most Food Brands.* Available at: https://ourfuture.org/20170105/oxfam-ten-multinational-corporations-control-most-food-brands (Accessed: 3 February 2018)

Jones, D. (2012) *Who cares wins: Why good business is better business.* Pearson UK.

Lii, Y.S. and Lee, M. (2012) Doing right leads to doing well: When the type of CSR and reputation interact to affect consumer evaluations of the firm. *Journal of business ethics,* 105(1), pp.69-81.

Linden, S, v, d. (2015) *The Psychology of Competition.* Available at: https://www.psychologytoday.com/blog/socially-relevant/201506/the-psychology-competition (Accessed: 5 January 2018)

Luckman, S. (2015) Craft and the Contemporary Cultural Economy: The Renaissance of the Handmade. *Craft and the Creative Economy* (pp. 1-11). Palgrave Macmillan, London.

M&S (2017) *Plan A 2025 Commitments.* Available at: http://planareport.marksandspencer.com/Plan_A_2025_Commitments.pdf (Accessed: 1 February 2018)

M&S (2018) *Supplier Management.* Available at: https://corporate.marksandspencer.com/plan-a/clothing-and-home/supplier-management#c1c128d936804a47834a5a787381c310 (Accessed: 26 January 2018)

M&S (2018) *Plan A Awards.* Available at: https://corporate.marksandspencer.com/plan-a/delivering-plan-a/plan-a-awards (Accessed: 3 February 2018)

Macleod, S. (2010) *CSR is no longer a 'bolt-on' activity.* Available at: https://www.theguardian.com/sustainable-business/blog/csr-corporate-social-responsibility (Accessed: 29 January 2018)

Manning, P. (2004) *Slavery, colonialism and economic growth in Dahomey,* 1640-1960 (Vol. 30). Cambridge University Press.

Mark, J. (2010) *Heraclitus of Ephesus.* Available at: https://www.ancient.eu/Heraclitus_of_Ephesos/ (Accessed: 7 January 2018)

Matten, D. and Moon, J. (2008) "Implicit" and "explicit" CSR: A conceptual framework for a comparative understanding of corporate social responsibility. *Academy of management Review*, 33(2), pp.404-424.

McKie, R. (2002) *Is human evolution finally over?* Available at: https://www.theguardian.com/science/2002/feb/03/genetics.research (Accessed: 5 January 2018)

Merchant, B. (2017) *Life and death in Apple's forbidden city.* Available at: https://www.theguardian.com/technology/2017/jun/18/foxconn-life-death-forbidden-city-longhua-suicide-apple-iphone-brian-merchant-one-device-extract (Accessed: 6 January 2018)

Merchant, B. (2017) *Were the raw materials in your iPhone mined by children in inhumane conditions?* Available at: http://www.latimes.com/opinion/op-ed/la-oe-merchant-iphone-supplychain-20170723-story.html (Accessed: 6 January 2018)

Mitroff, I. (1983) Stakeholders of the organizational mind. *Jossey-Bass Inc Pub.*

Mohan, B., Norton, M.I. and Deshpande, R. (2015) Paying up for fair pay: Consumers prefer firms with lower CEO-to-worker pay ratios.

Moore, M. (2012) *'Mass suicide' protest at Apple manufacturer Foxconn factory.* Available at: http://www.telegraph.co.uk/news/worldnews/asia/china/9006988/Mass-suicide-protest-at-Apple-manufacturer-Foxconn-factory.html (Accessed: 7 January 2018)

Morely, N. (2017) *Tesco vows to give all edible leftovers to charity.* Available at: http://metro.co.uk/2017/12/23/tesco-vows-give-edible-leftovers-charity-7181706/ (Accessed: 2 February 2018)

Neilson (2013) *Nielsen: 50% Of Global Consumers Surveyed Willing To Pay More For Goods, Services From Socially Responsible Companies, Up From 2011.* Available at: http://www.nielsen.com/uk/en/press-room/2013/nielsen-50-percent-of-global-consumers-surveyed-willing-to-pay-more-fo.html (Accessed: 12 February 2018)

Neilson (2015) *The Sustainability Imperative.* Available at: http://www.nielsen.com/us/en/insights/reports/2015/the-sustainability-imperative.html (Accessed: 24 January 2018)

Norton, M. and Avery, J. (2011) *The Pepsi Refresh Project: A Thirst for Change.*

O'Boyle, E.H., Patel, P.C. and Gonzalez-Mulé, E. (2016) Employee ownership and firm performance: a meta-analysis. *Human Resource Management Journal,* 26(4), pp.425-448.

O'Donovan, C. (2017) *Here's How Apple Is Doing On Conflict Minerals.* Available at: https://www.buzzfeed.com/carolineodonovan/apple-reports-conflict-mineral-progress-as-president-trump?utm_term=.lsLmmmNB6#.ombAAA3z0 (Accessed: 23 January 2018)

ONS (2017) *Business demography, UK: 2016.* Available at: https://www.ons.gov.uk/businessindustryandtrade/business/activitysizeandlocation/bulletins/businessdemography/2016 (Accessed: 15 January 2018)

Oswald, A.J., Proto, E. and Sgroi, D. (2015) Happiness and productivity. *Journal of Labor Economics,* 33(4), pp.789-822.

PepsiCo (2018) *Performance with Purpose.* Available at: http://www.pepsico.com/sustainability/Performance-with-Purpose (Accessed: 21 February 2018)

Popper, N. (2015) *Digital gold: Bitcoin and the inside story of the misfits and millionaires trying to reinvent money* (pp. 156-197). New York: Harper.

Primark (2018) *Our Ethics.* Available at: https://www.primark.com/en/our-ethics/frequently-asked-questions (Accessed: 1 February 2018)

Quinn, J.J. (1997) Personal ethics and business ethics: The ethical attitudes of owner/managers of small business. *Journal of Business Ethics,* 16(2), pp.119-127.

Rudominer, R. (2017) *Corporate Social Responsibility Matters: Ignore Millennials at Your Peril.* Available at: https://www.huffingtonpost.com/ryan-rudominer/corporate-social-responsi_9_b_9155670.html (Accessed: 7 February 2018)

Rumbold, A. (2014) *30 year study shows social ventures more likely to survive than PLCs.* Available at: https://www.theguardian.com/social-enterprise-network/2014/jun/10/social-enterprises-are-unstable (Accessed: 16 February 2018)

Sandel, M.J. (2012) *What money can't buy: the moral limits of markets.* Macmillan.

Sanders, B. (2017) *Do we really see 4,000 ads a day?* Available at: https://www.bizjournals.com/bizjournals/how-to/marketing/2017/09/do-we-really-see-4-000-ads-a-day.html (Accessed: 23 February 2018)

Starbucks (no date) *Starbucks Shared Planet.* Availablae at: https://mena.starbucks.com/MENA/en/newsroomarticle/sections/about-starbucks/starbucks-shared-planet.html (Accessed 17 February 2018)

Statistia (2017) *Apple's number of employees in the fiscal years 2005 to 2017 (in 1,000s).* Available at: https://www.statista.com/statistics/273439/number-of-employees-of-apple-since-2005/ (Accessed: 4 January 2018)

Stoet, G. and Geary, D.C. (2018) The Gender-Equality Paradox in Science, Technology, Engineering, and Mathematics Education. *Psychological science,* p.95

The Body Shop (2018) *Ban Animal Testing.* Available at: https://www.thebodyshop.com/en-gb/about-us/against-animal-testing (Accessed: 20 January 2018)

Thornicroft, G., Rose, D., Kassam, A. and Sartorius, N. (2007) *Stigma: ignorance, prejudice or discrimination?.*

Titcomb, J. (2017) *Apple's cash reserves swell to $250bn.* Available at: http://www.telegraph.co.uk/technology/2017/05/01/apples-cash-reserves-swell-250bn/ (Accessed: 8 January 2018)

Truxillo, D.M., Finkelstein, L.M., Pytlovany, A.C. and Jenkins, J.S. (2015) Age discrimination at work: a review of the research and recommendations for the future. *Oxford handbook of workplace discrimination.* Oxford University Press.

Tsesis, A. (2014) The right to erasure: Privacy, data brokers, and the indefinite retention of data. *Wake Forest L. Rev.,* 49, p.433.

Unilever (2018) *1960 - 1969: A time for growth.* Available at: https://www.unilever.co.uk/about/who-we-are/our-history/1960-1969.html (Accessed: 1 February 2018)

Unilever (2018) *Our Strategy for Sustainable Business.* Available at: https://www.unilever.com/sustainable-living/our-strategy/ (Accessed: 30 January 2018)

Unilever (2018) *Sustainable Living.* Available at: https://www.unilever.co.uk/sustainable-living/ (Accessed: 6 February 2018)

Urry, M (2008) *Primark Takes Action Over Child Labour.* Available at: https://www.ft.com/content/7821ffdc-3bd8-11dd-9cb2-0000779fd2ac (Accessed: 27 January 2018)

Varadarajan, P.R. and Menon, A. (1988) Cause-related marketing: A coalignment of marketing strategy and corporate philanthropy. *The Journal of Marketing*, pp.58-74.

Wahl, D, C. (2017) *Evolution Shows Collaboration, not Competition, Helped us Evolve.* Available at: https://upliftconnect.com/collaboration-not-competition-helped-us-evolve/ (Accessed: 18 January 2018)

Walt, V. (2017) *Unilever CEO Paul Polman's Plan to Save the World.* Available at: http://fortune.com/2017/02/17/unilever-paul-polman-responsibility-growth/ (Accessed: 9 February 2018)

Wattle, J. (2018) *More than a dozen businesses ran away from the NRA.* Available at: http://money.cnn.com/2018/02/25/news/companies/companies-abandoning-nra-list/index.html (Accessed: 25 February 2018)

Westervelt, A. (2015) *Two years after Rana Plaza, have conditions improved in Bangladesh's factories?* Available at: https://www.theguardian.com/sustainable-business/2015/apr/24/bangladesh-factories-building-collapse-garment-dhaka-rana-plaza-brands-hm-gap-workers-construction (Accessed: 4 February 2018)

Wongpitch, S., Minakan, N., Powpaka, S. and Laohavichien, T., (2016) Effect of corporate social responsibility motives on purchase intention model: An extension. *Kasetsart Journal of Social Sciences*, 37(1), pp.30-37.

Xiu, L. and Gunderson, M. (2014) Glass ceiling or sticky floor? Quantile regression decomposition of the gender pay gap in China. *International Journal of Manpower*, 35(3), pp.306-326.